IT'S YOU

THE ACTOR, THE DECIDER, THE RESPONDER

SANJEEVANI CHATTERJEE

"To the me that needed to hear these words. And to those who want to change the way they feel by changing the way they think"

Contents

Contents

Contents

Contents

Contents

Preface

Beginning a new journey, I guess. So the question is: What inspired me? Philosophy and the way of living. Philosophy is a subject that interests you enough to delve deep into it. It is not boring; it just questions you, your thoughts, your existence, reasoning,choice, knowledge, value, and your mind. It is an activity that people go through when they want to understand the fundamental truths about themselves and their relationship to the world and to each other. One of my favourite philosophies is Stoicism, which revolves around every person and teaches the development of self-control as a means of overcoming destructive emotions. It allows us to be unbiased thinkers in order to get to a certain point. I wasn't aware of the fact earlier that stoicism can be used as a tool for wisdom,self-mastery, and perseverance.

With passing time, I have observed that what we read and hear shapes our perception of life, so I can say that every person has some theories that provide them with the needed strength and motivation for their daily challenges. Stoicism, for me, is one of them. This states that virtue (virtues of self-control, courage, justice, and wisdom) is happiness. Our perception of things is the reason that we get so much affected. So, it is not them, but you. We are humans, and we will encounter different experiences in our lives, some good, some bad, and some surprises, but it all depends on our ability to use our reason to choose how we see the event, observe it, categorise it, respond to it, and change our response. There are several instances where I can say that I made the right decision by simply being aware of my thoughts and responding to the event instead of reacting.

Suppose there is a fertile field where logic is the protective fence, physics is the field, and the crop that all this is producing is ethics, or a guiding force on how to live. This, we can say, is analogous to the philosophy of Stoics. We must have read various solutions to our questions relating to what we are, who we are, why we behave the way we do, why there is anger, why jealousy, and many more. But this philosophy came up with practicable answers revolving around how we perceive or see the world around us; it depends on our perception of things; how we take decisions and what actions we take based on our perception of events; and how we deal with things we cannot change or the things upon which we do not have any control. And knowing all this, how can we come to a conclusion and attain a clear understanding of ourselves? That is how, by controlling our perceptions, we will find clarity. By understanding our actions and analysing them, we will be effective and productive, and by utilising our willpower, we will have the strength to deal with anything the world puts before us. We must cultivate within ourselves the resilience, purpose, and joy of living every day as all days.

We are living a life where some are happy, some are stressed, some do not know what they are doing, some are confused, some are enjoying their days, some are overburdened with work, some are active, some are lazy, some are just living their life with purpose or with no purpose, some are just bored, and huhh! The list goes on and on. I want to thank Ryan Holiday and Stephen Hanselman because, when I read "The Daily Stoic," I gained a very different vision altogether, and this motivated me to write something. So whatever it is, I believe that this book will help you to relax and will give you a perspective on how important your thoughts are and how they can impact your well-being. I hope in this book you will get to know an amazing side regarding our thoughts and how it impacts our perception, how our perception defines us, and the benefits of controlling our perception by controlling our thoughts in order to get a life that is not as unorganised as we think. So cheers to a better life!

CHAPTER I

BE GRATEFUL

The world is not a dark place to be; it is a beautiful place. It is just a matter of perspective. When we focus on the brighter side of life, we will see the world exactly like the way we feel. There are so many positive things in life. It can be anything that makes you feel good. Spending time with your loved ones, enjoying nature, pursuing hobbies, helping others, and experiencing moments of joy and laughter. It is all about finding happiness—a feeling where you are just yourself, carefree, and in the moment. Be grateful for everything. You are really lucky to be sitting in a place with the command of your life in your own hands.

Being grateful is such an amazing mindset to have because it lets us appreciate the good things that we have in our lives and focus on what we have rather than what we lack. It can bring so much positivity into our lives. Isn't it wonderful how we are able to change our mindset by just changing our thoughts, by just re-interpreting our thoughts,by just changing the way we think or approach things? So take a moment every day to be grateful for all the things that you have. When I was a kid, I used to read poems and think about how the writer thought—so deep yet so mesmerising. I asked my mother *how the poet is so optimistic and how he is able to look at nature or everyday activities with so much grace and enthusiasm.* She replied, *We all should see the world like them only. Seeing the world as a poet allows us to appreciate the beauty and wonder in everyday moments. They have a very unique way of observing the world, finding inspiration in the simplest things, and expressing their emotions through words. It feels like looking at the world through a creative lens, where even the ordinary becomes extraordinary. Try to behave that way, girl. It's a beautiful way to see and experience the joys of life.*

CHAPTER II

JUST START

Everyone wants to live a free life, a life where fear doesn't exist, a life where we are miles away from greed and anger, a life where we are consistently growing, a life where we have no ill feelings for others, a life where we are satisfied and happy, and a life where we believe in God and in that power who is taking care of us. We just have to practise all these things, but why do we fail? Do we fail because we are afraid of even trying to feel this way, only thinking about what if we fail?

We are surrounded by people who are living their lives half-heartedly and have an excuse ready. But as we grow older, we realise that this feeling where people want to live a free life, a life where fear doesn't exist, a life where we are miles away from greed and anger, a life where we are consistently growing, a life where we have no ill feelings for others, a life where we are satisfied,where we are happy, and where we believe in God, in that power who is taking care of us, is really required if we want to improve the quality of our life and if we want to improve our ability to deal with the world around us. Having an attitude like this will solve most of our problems.

So, do not worry. Just start working on yourself, on your thoughts, observing your thought patterns, and see how you are responding to them. Meditate, spend time with yourself, and just begin somewhere; the rest always follows.

CHAPTER III

DO ONE THING AT A TIME

Why are we in a hurry? Why do we want to do everything at once? Why are we not patient? Why do we constantly try to make things complex? Why aren't we happy in our simple lives, or do we want a simple life but are always ready to complicate it? If you see, life is simple; we are the ones making it complicated with our own perceptions, judgements, and actions. I know it takes a lot to react normally when a situation doesn't go in our favour, but it is what it is. Rushing will do no good. If we are given work, we must focus on each task because, in life, our duties are the sum of individual tasks. We just need to focus on each step and then move forward. We can't just think about the conclusion while writing the introduction. If we do that, our introduction will not be the best. Whenever we are assigned a task or, generally in life, whenever we find ourselves reluctant to do some work because of personal tensions, we can think, Are our own interpersonal tensions really bigger than the work? Or there is nothing unreasonable in what they are asking us to do. These kinds of situations often arise between you and your boss, between you and your mindset, or between you and someone else, but just do your work, one thing at a time, and you will realise that pretty soon you have done the entire thing.

Do not make things harder than they need to be because of your own personal reasons. Be present in the moment—in this very moment. Life is tough, but so are you. Just try not to get emotional in between your work; try not to put your emotions into insignificant things. Try to keep things simple; see what is there; don't assume; focus on what you are doing now—no past, no future, just now. A simple life is a beautiful life. We overthink, but in reality, there is something good in every moment. Keep your focus there.

CHAPTER IV

WHEREVER YOU ARE, BE ALL THERE

Most of the time, we keep ourselves indulged in the past or present. We think, Oh! My past was so different; it was a good time; why did that incident happen; will I get to experience the same fun again; and the list goes on and on. Or we think, What will happen? Am I going to lead a life earning this much salary? Will I have friends? How will my colleague behave with me? And this list of "wills" goes on and on. But we don't think about the time we are wasting in thinking about these things; we are ignoring our present moment, which is the most precious thing we can use for so many productive things. But see, what are we doing? We are not even present in the present moment; we are still figuring out what has happened or what will happen. I wonder sometimes: why is it so tough to be in the present moment?

Your life is your own; no one can live your life better than you. There are people whose present has a different meaning than yours, but it is still a present. Utilise it wisely. No individual can have the same life, the same upbringing, or the same bank balance, so is there a point in thinking about these things and wasting your life? I don't think so, so be happy with what you have, make yourself a person who appreciates their present, and try to build each present day with all the energy you have because your present can last a whole lifetime as every day is a present, and it depends on you how you are using it.

Just think: if you only had this time, this moment, would you go through the same thought that you constantly make yourself go through, or are there better things in life to be grateful for? Enjoy your present, and it will be enough. Always ask yourself, *Are you happy at this moment? What is disturbing you at this very moment?* and you will see the difference. Everything eventually falls back to its place, so it is better to enjoy the journey as it comes, and it is always better to live in the moment, so wherever you are, be all there.

CHAPTER V

ACKNOWLEDGE YOUR KNOWLEDGE

No one can take "what you know" from you. No matter where you go or what you do, your skills and knowledge are going to stay with you. You can always upskill yourself. There are times when we feel lost, when we don't know what our purpose is, and when we don't know what we are going to do. But one thing we all must know is that it is just a part of us thinking this way, but when this part calms down, we will again be ready to go. Change the way you feel. If you feel like you are depressed and you are good for nothing, then tell yourself: *You are not feeling depressed; you are not inactive; you are not dumb; it is just that part of your soul feeling this way.* The moment they feel better, you will soon realise it was just your mood at that very time. You are a strong being; you must know that.

We all make mistakes, we all feel low, and we all encounter questions like, What is next? But this is it. This has nothing to do with the knowledge we have; this doesn't mean that we have lost our intelligence or our skills. You are still a wise person; our knowledge and skills are just on hold; they are not affected by our current situation. You paused a little; you will start again. And you will start stronger because what is for you will come back to you. Trust yourself and be self-assured, because what you can bring to the table, no one else can bring.

CHAPTER VI

OUR OPINION MATTERS

Do you have an opinion on today's weather? Do you have an opinion about the girl sitting beside you? Do you have an opinion on the dressing sense of other people? Do you have an opinion about people who don't think like you? Do you have an opinion on someone's way of saying something? Do you have an opinion when someone doesn't behave the way you want them to? Yes, we have opinions on each and everything. Everyone has an opinion. So why do you get angry when someone's thoughts don't match yours? Everyone is unique; they can have different opinions. If it is your right to make stories, it's their right too. Coming back to the point, we are constantly looking around us and putting our opinions on it. We don't think about whether the matters are worth our opinions or not. We just have it; after all, it's free.

But don't you think our opinions are a combination of several factors? Either they are dominated by our religious and cultural beliefs, by some kind of expectation, or, in some cases, by the knowledge we see in the media. Our opinions are not always right, but they are ours. So we have the power to make changes. If you find yourself sad or angry most of the time, ask yourself: Is it because of my opinions on certain matters that don't get executed as I wanted them to? But what if we try to change our opinions? What if we try to understand whether the situation is really impacting us or if it's just our opinion on that? Why do you get affected when an influencer travels the world? Why do you get affected when someone you barely know doesn't say 'hi' to you? Why are you affected when the friends you made do not react the way you wanted?

Why do you have opinions on everything? Why can't you let things just be as they are without complicating it with your opinions? Opinions always create a certain kind of emotion that you can feel, so your body reacts in that way. Why can't we just try to see things as they are—not good, not bad—just as they are? You will realise that when you shift your opinions to only those matters that really belong to you, that can have an impact on you, and that lie in the field of your own choice, you will achieve something very amazing irrespective of whatever is happening around you, and that is your peace of mind.

CHAPTER VII

KNOW THE DIFFERENCE

Nothing is permanent; live a life where you know nothing is going to be with you forever. Things may disappear, but knowing how to be happy and calm is the real mantra. You have money now; who knows, you will have money forever? You are thin now; who knows you will be thin? There is nothing that will stay with you forever. You must see where you are putting your attention. I really admire such people who love materialistic things, but at the same time, they know that these are just things that are not going to stay with them forever, and they plan their lives accordingly. Just imagine how powerful you will be in a place where everyone else is busy stressing over their perfect weight, money, and situations, and for you, these things don't matter so much. You will feel the power within yourself where everyone else is upset most of the time, some are stressed, a few are overexcited, overly possessive, greedy, or angry, and you, on the other hand, are objective, calm, composed, and have clarity in mind. Imagine the amount of peace you will have with yourself, your family, friends, and colleagues.

It all begins with ourselves; our mood decides our day. Our beliefs shape our attitudes. Change is the only constant thing, and we must go with the flow, as it is not always about ignoring or avoiding the situation; it is more about not giving so much importance to the things that do not need so much importance. Know the difference.

CHAPTER VIII

CONDITIONAL HAPPINESS

Happiness and conditional happiness are not at all compatible. Happiness is independent; conditional happiness is dependent. Our happiness should not depend on anything. Real happiness is only felt when we don't set any conditions. It only depends on our mental attitude. We can't say, *I will be happy if I get this, I will be happy once I get this job, I will be happy when my life gets sorted,I will wear new clothes when I get a job, I will be happy when ...* happiness doesn't work like this. Life is never going to be sorted out; setting conditions for happiness is like walking endlessly without a path or a destination where we are not even getting closer to happiness.

Always thinking about what lies ahead, imagining something we desire, and looking forward to some great happy moments—these activities seem pleasurable, but they ruin our chances of being happy at this moment because we are scheduling our happiness. Conditional happiness comes in between our personal growth, as it prevents us from being happy in the moment. Your words have power, so instead of saying "*I will be happy when,*" say "*I am happy now, happy in this moment.*" Sooner or later, you will realise being happy is the greatest form of success.

CHAPTER IX

LIFE'S BANQUET

Their life is so good. I too want this; why am I here as a loser? I want to achieve whatever she has, and I too want this. We often find people who are not happy with what they have, and they continuously crib about it. They always want what others have; they ignore how grateful they should be. Whenever you find yourself in a mood where you can do anything to get what someone else has, just remind yourself—it's bad manners to take someone else's portion. Wait for your turn; you will get whatever is destined for you. Just work hard and do good. No one can take your shares from you; you will get everything that is in your part. God is kind; he is looking upon you. Be patient and wait for your turn.

I really like the analogy of Epictetus' metaphor of *life's banquet*. So life is like a banquet, where there are varieties of food but not everybody eats the same food. Everyone has their own choices, their own tastes, and their own needs. There is nothing to compare. It doesn't matter to which section you are invited. The thing that matters is actually choosing what you want to have and being happy about it. You can also see this example from a different point of view, where it teaches us the basic values of being grateful, as we are so lucky that we are getting this chance to choose what we want and we are invited to such a big feast; it teaches us how to enjoy the present moment by focusing on what is on our plate at that very moment; it also teaches us that when things end, it is our duty to clean up the mess selflessly; and it also teaches charity that the next time we are in charge, we have this responsibility to do good things for others. So plan accordingly, because it is really not about what you have. It is always about how you are enjoying life in general, with your own definition of happiness.

CHAPTER X

WE CANNOT HAVE IT ALL

I still remember the time when my family used to sit together and discuss the general stuff—actually, the most important stuff—that revolved around the topic of "the way of living your life." In the discussion, every individual shared their perspective about what their priorities are, how they choose between two options, how they are dealing with their mindset, and whether they are clear or still figuring out their ways of living. I miss those days. Now everyone is so busy with other things that they have forgotten the meaning of these little discussions that can make a huge impact. There are people who believe we can have it all, but we cannot have it all. Because our desires and wants are never-ending. We can have a nice, loving family, a good earning source, and a healthy body, but we will still crave more. Not all humans are content with their lives. We are and will always be cluttered with so many thoughts and so many choices. No one wants less; everyone wants to do everything. But is this possible? There will be something that you cannot do. And it is completely okay. Keep trying, while at the same time training your mind to prioritise things. No individual can be happy if they set their heart on so many things. Schedule weekly meetings with yourself and get the answers to so many important questions, like what do you want? What do you have to do in order to get there? What is stopping you? What are your distractions? What are the things that are not adding any value to your profile? What will happen if things do not go according to your plan, etc. And this can go on and on.

Be honest with your answers; you are the only person there; no one will judge you; accept that you will not get everything as per your wish, but God's plan is always the best, I guess. Coming back to the point, talk it out, talk to yourself, and the answers will definitely give you a clear perspective about the things you should focus on and about the things that you can ignore. This will help you relax, make you more productive in your approach, help you cut out all the unnecessary things where you are involved, and make you value your time more efficiently.

CHAPTER XI

ANGER IS A TRAP

Have you ever thought being driven by your anger could be beneficial for someone who doesn't like you? Or maybe your anger is a by-product of their behaviour, and they know you so well that they control you whenever they want to. Anger, love, lust, unhappiness—these are all just feelings that are created by our own perception. There are many rules created to control your anger, but the one most famous is: whenever you feel that your body is reacting to something generating a feeling of anger, try to count till five slowly, one, two, three, four, and then see the difference. We always react instantly when we feel angry, and sooner or later, we regret what we did. Anger can trigger a feeling of shame, especially when we express it in ways that go against our values and moral systems. We sometimes say things we don't even mean to people we love, but later we feel ashamed. So if you think anger makes you a macho person, it does not. The more you go towards a calmer mind, the stronger you become.

There are people who try to provoke us by saying things that have the power to trigger us. Anger makes us weak. We often see these kinds of activities in the playground where the player says offensive and nasty things to their competitors in order to get a reaction and to distract them. Anger is a big mistake. It destroys our capacity to perform better at work or in life too. Generally, we find ourselves in a trap of our anger that may be or may not be created by others in order to destroy our peace. But we need to keep one thing in mind: anger only distracts us; it harms our mental well-being, sometimes physical too. So keep anger under your control; do not get controlled by anger. If you want to shine high and lead a happy and peaceful life, you need strength. And strength can only be attained if you go close to a calmer mind, away from anger.

Strength is the ability to maintain a hold of oneself. The person who does not crib, the person who never gets mad, the person who is so strong-headed that they know what turning hot-headed will lead them to, the person with clarity of thought, and the person with a calmer mindset live a happy and healthy life. Choose wisely; you can either control your anger or get controlled by it. Your reaction always depends on you.

CHAPTER XII

ANXIETY

Sometimes I wonder: What if I stop taking stress? Sometimes, when I am happy, I wonder: How long will this last? Sometimes, when everything goes right, I doubt it. We are so used to being anxious that we have forgotten that it is just an emotion. Being anxious is a feeling that is in our control. But why do we get anxious? I guess because we wanted something and didn't get it as expected, or because we created something in our own minds and it is not happening the way we expected it to, we get anxious because we always want something that is not in our control. This is a loop where we know we are being anxious about things that aren't in our control and still think about them and damage our mental well-being. Everyone is stressed and has proper reasons to be stressed, but I don't think there is a reason to be stressed. If you are having an exam, you should give your best. Just give your best, and the outcome is not in your hands. So why take stress? If you are planning to go somewhere and you don't have adequate money, try to work harder and ask yourself: Will being anxious give me money or can it give me a headache that will cost more money?

There are many examples that you can think of where, eventually, you will realise that being anxious doesn't solve any of the problems. Being in the moment and having a calmer mindset will keep us away from anxiety. Try to sit with yourself without doing anything and observe your thoughts. To get something you want, you must sacrifice your peace of mind; this is not how it works. Whenever you find yourself constantly thinking about some event, some people, or something that is making you anxious, knock yourself up and ask yourself: Why are you thinking this? Does it make any sense? Is it doing any good? Is it really required? It sounds silly, but I have done this, and it works. You will get a hold of your anxiety, and you will decide whether you want to be anxious or not. It's all in your control.

CHAPTER XIII

ARE OUR DESIRES VICES?

The world is full of dichotomies. There are people who say drugs are bad; don't do it, and there are people who say drugs are cool. If you don't do it, you will have fewer people around you. But if you are into such activities, then you are surrounded by people. It all depends on us and the perspective with which people judge each other. Every individual has desires—something that they enjoy doing and want to do. Some may have a desire for travelling, trekking, reading books, spending time with friends, drinking, having good sex, etc. There is nothing wrong with that. Problems arise when someone tells you what your desire should be, when they try to enforce their desire on you, and when the desires are harmful or can become an addiction. Our desires are vices or virtues; it only depends on us, and this should be limited to those that are in our control and not influenced by external surroundings. Anyone can get influenced or addicted to anything, anywhere, so be mindful of your choices. Always think about it the next time you have a craving or are thinking about engaging in a harmless vice!

CHAPTER XIV

ARE WE REALLY INDEPENDENT AND SELF SUFFICIENT?

We don't like it when someone tries to control us. We hate being controlled. We don't like it when we have to do things that others want. We hate accepting orders from others. We don't like when someone tells us how to dress or how to live. We hate it when someone tries to be our boss. We always want to argue with them and prove our points right. But why do we do these things? We consider ourselves to be self-sufficient and independent individuals. A person who can take care of themselves, someone who does not need anyone's opinion on how they should live. We are confident in what we do. Yes, we are independent beings; we are self-sufficient, but does this make us happy? If the answer is no, then ask yourself why. Self-sufficiency and independence are the gifts that we must remain grateful for. But regardless of having the power to be self-sufficient, we misuse the power by reacting to our impulses. Have you ever thought that if you had the knowledge that someone else was trying to control your life, then you must know what you are trying to do with yourself?

There are times when we are the ones questioning our duties, self-sufficiency, and independence. We are the ones who act as barriers in our own paths. Why don't we try to control our impulses if we are so active and aware of what others are trying to do? If we are not ready to challenge our own impulses, how can we be ready to fight with others? A proper frame of mind is necessary where you know that you are not under any control, where you are not controlled by other people or even by your own emotions, where you stop complaining about what people did, and where you start to look beyond all of this, where you won't let yourselves be enslaved by your inner demons. Act smart, because no one can make an impact or hurt you if you do not give them that power. I know it is easier said than done, but we have to make ourselves so strong that we should be the ones in control, not our emotions, because, as we always say, we are independent and self-sufficient people.

CHAPTER XV

ARE YOU A VICTIM?

Have you cried and said, "She is so bad?" Have you ever bitched about your boss? Have you ever felt that your boss is so irritating, your life is so boring, or everyone is ignoring you? Or how can they treat you like this? Or have you ever cribbed about a person everywhere? Have you ever blamed someone else for your sadness? Have you ever blamed situations that didn't work out as you wished? Have you ever reacted without understanding the scenario? In short, have you ever played a blame game and tried to portray yourself as a victim? If the answer is yes, then what I am going to say will make you think about it. I know it is tough—really tough—to not play a victim card whenever a person or situation shows their side. But the fact is, it is not the other person or some situation that has the power in themselves to make us feel the way they want us to feel. The problem and frustration always lie in our own assumptions and expectations. I know it is a very difficult thing to adapt to, but if you want to be at peace, you must understand this.

Earlier, I used to blame situations and people, but now I understand, they did what they felt was right. I should not hurt myself by constantly thinking about them. I should respect myself. There will be things that do not work out, but that does not mean our lives have ended. If you want to be at peace, forgive everyone and move on. It is no one's fault; it just didn't happen, and that's it. Don't complicate it much. No one except you has the power to frustrate you; it is your responsibility to create a single key for accessing your mind, and that key should always remain with you. The emotions that you feel are all your creation. They are coming from inside; they are just dependent on external factors, but make yourself so strong that you can become someone who can differentiate between the emotions that are externally dependent and the power that you have over them. The other side always becomes the target, but the real cause lies within us. Observe some people who have full control over their thoughts and emotions, and see how they respond to every situation. Try to learn from them; you will surely get motivated. Because it is not right to blame someone else for your worry and frustration, as they did their part. Let them be with their deeds; you have to take care of yourself, and it can only be done if you change your perspective.

Remember, the cause is always within us; it can be external, but the way we choose to deal with that externally created stress and the amount to which we are triggered always depends on us. And it has been said many times that it is all you. Everyone has a choice—their own choice. You are the one in charge at all times. The source of our stress, our frustration, our irritation, or our perception that something is wrong is within us. And it is happening only because of our values, opinions, and expectations. If this is happening to us because of our own expectations, then it is also upon us to easily change those labels, as well as our expectations and attitude towards them, and to choose to accept and appreciate the world around us. So choose your reaction wisely because your reaction can be dependent on external things, but it is impossible to get your reaction activated without your consent.

CHAPTER XVI

ARE YOU REALLY BEAUTIFUL?

People are so busy in their lives, in their careers, in their relationships, and in all the matters that they are involved in that they forget that these are just a part of their whole life. These are not their lives. We tend to confuse our parts of life with our whole lives. But life has much more to offer. I have seen that most people have lost their basic sense of understanding the meaning of life. They are doing whatever is good for their presence in society without thinking about themselves or the impact they are creating in their lives. They are so confused about things that they forgot: earlier, people used to earn money to live their lives, but now people are living their lives to earn money. Earlier, people used to work hard to reach a place where they could be proud of themselves, but now people are trying to reach a place just to show others first, and they are also not happy as they are comparing themselves with their peers. They have lost the sense of choosing between what is the right path. We all need to understand that if we are individuals who are known for our ability to choose wisely, then we are in a very respectable place. But if we think we are known for our job, for the bank balance, or for the materialistic things we possess, then, my dear, we are all thinking wrong. It is our ability to present ourselves; the way we behave and the way we choose are what make us beautiful. You are not defined by the work you are doing; you are known for the way you treat yourself and people; you are known for the way you put your values and opinions in front of people.

You are known by the way you are; your original identity is not dependent on anything else except yourself. We always judge people by the way they appear, but is this the right criteria for making a judgement? No. Before going down this line, make yourself aware of the fact that things are not the way they appear; there is a lot behind it. Try to see from where they are coming, what are their choices, and what led them to be here; that will make a huge difference, not their appearance or any other thing attached to or related to them. It is just you who can make the difference; it is difficult but not impossible. Everything you are comes from your choices, and this is the real beauty.

CHAPTER XVII

AWARENESS OR EDUCATION

There are times when we feel people who are actually educated are not so well educated, and an illiterate person who understands the basic reality of nature and what our role as individuals is is far more respectable. They are backing up their ability with their awareness. If you are an individual who is very well read but is unable to channel your knowledge in the right direction, and you do not know what being truly aware of yourself and your knowledge means, then what is the point of getting that degree? There are many things that are above education, and that is, what are your values, how you perceive your surroundings, how you treat other people, what are your personality traits, are you honest, are you a sadist, or who are you and what do you want?

We all have common sense. I am saying this, but it is a rare thing to find. I know a boy who was not good at studying but is making a lot of money because of his business skills, and the most important thing is that he was aware of his strengths and weaknesses. On the other hand, there are his friends who are engineers but are not at all happy with their lives. So it is really important to know what you want to do, as being properly educated means knowing how we are applying what we know and whether we are able to separate the things that lie within our control from those that don't.

Experience is the only thing that gives meaning to the words. Only studying and not applying things will do no good. Experience is the best teacher. There is a theory behind everything that you can understand only by experiencing. And that is why nowadays a lot of emphasis is placed on practical learning. Without your experience and your ability to take action, no theory or no knowledge can help you get out of your comfort zone. Studying is very important, but it can also become effective when you truly comprehend the meaning behind what you are studying. Living your life is the best teacher that will give you different kinds of experiences. The only way left to determine if you are applying the lessons is to look back on your actions, decisions, and behaviours over time. Remember, everything that you do, be it going to work, saying 'hi' to fellow mates, giving a tip, or having a conversation, all comes from your experiences and what you see around you. Take the most out of education by being aware, as education is the training of the mind to think. Its goal is to increase awareness, widen our horizons of thinking, and watch our inner responses and how we are responding.

CHAPTER XVIII

ATTENTION PLEASE

Why do you get distracted? What is happening? Do you think multitasking has reduced your capacity to focus on one task at a time? No one has created something amazing when they were just roaming around multitasking. Great things always come when you focus and give your attention to the required task. I have seen many people who think they can manage their home, their government exam preparation, their relationships, their travel, and their parties. Only a few can do that. Otherwise, it is a very difficult task. I believe that wherever we are and whatever we do, paying attention or being there is necessary. Without being there fully or without paying attention, what is the point of doing that? I have seen people who are in their class but are thinking about what they will wear at today's party. We are living a life where we are not paying our full attention to the activities we do, where we are getting distracted by every new app, social media, notifications, book, tweets, messages, posts, and whatnot. When I started writing this, I used to get distracted thinking about whether I had received any messages, whether I should see that video, whether I had to call someone, and whether I would be able to complete this book or not. All these things occupied my mind when I was busy doing my work. And all the distractions are, in some way or another, related to our thoughts.

Doing things half-heartedly doesn't make any sense; you will feel a different vibe when you decide to give it your all. Building attention is a habit, and getting yourself distracted is a mistake, as now that you have kept yourself engaged in more than one thing, that will affect your mind and will take more time to complete. No one can complete all their tasks if they allow themselves to get distracted every time there is any kind of interruption. Our mind is the only thing that is completely ours, and every task of ours is dependent on it. So it is our responsibility to pay attention to what our mind thinks as we become what we think we are. It is our duty to keep our minds free and clear so that they can focus on what's truly necessary. Our attention is one of our biggest strengths that we can use to make the most of all the work that we do. If you want to give someone or a task of yours a gift, give them your attention and your full presence, and trust me, it is the best gift that they will cherish forever.

CHAPTER XIX

BE PREPARED

32

We all must have a plan—a plan to deal with uncertain situations, a plan to prevent events that will impact us—even after knowing that situations that are going to arise may or may not be in our hands. We cannot control the events that will happen, but we can be prepared for them. We often hear people say, Hope for the best and prepare for the worst. This is how life works. Things don't always go according to our plans, but we must make ourselves so strong that even if situations don't go according to our plan, we can stand against all odds. In order to get a rainbow, we must pass through storms. There will be troubles in life, no matter how hard you try to avoid them, but troubles are unavoidable. The best you can do is to be prepared for their occurrence. Be prepared mentally and be ready for anything that comes your way.

CHAPTER XX

BEHAVE AS IF YOU ARE PLAYING A MATCH

Playing in a team teaches a lot; it teaches us to interact, to think about a larger perspective, and to think not only for ourselves but for all of us as a team. It makes us more understanding of what others must be going through. Or when playing against someone, we observe him, we try to know his moves, but at the same time, we don't hate him. We just try to know about him for our own good. We should act like this in our lives too, where we pay close attention to the people with whom we are interacting and spending most of our time with, while at the same time not developing any hard feelings for them. Like I said earlier, do your best, try to do good for others, and never try to harm them. But never chase people to be with you; if someone is happy without you, let them be. It is always possible to avoid people without hating them. Treat your life as a playground where you know what kind of mistakes you make so that you can be in a better position to understand the situations of other people.

Always remind yourself that you are a learning being, and so are your companions. If you can make mistakes, they can too. Your thoughts and your mind are loyal students; they behave as you tell them to behave. So try to be a good coach. Everyone is learning and trying to upgrade themselves; be a little understanding and empathetic.

CHAPTER XXI

CHANT

Words have a lot of power. Things that we say to ourselves really boost our confidence and mental well-being. Chanting a mantra, a saying, or the lyrics of an inspirational song can be our saviour whenever we are in a tough situation. We can always erase the negative thoughts that occupy our minds; it just requires replacing that thought with a powerful mantra or any saying of your choice. Human beings are such powerful creatures that they can do anything they wish for; they can think what they want to think and ignore things that do not matter, but wait,do we really make use of that power? Just try this once, whenever you find yourself in a tough situation, just say some affirmations like,*I am powerful, I am capable, I have the power to rock the world, I deserve peace, I am happy, I am focusing only on the things that matter, and I am not thinking about things that are not in my control.* You will see a difference. Everything is in our hands. Our reactions can make a difference. There are times when uttering a word or a phrase, having a thought, or even peaceful sounds can give us clarity and keep us at peace. Chanting or uttering something that gives you strength allows you to block out every negative thing that you are thinking about.

So know your powerful mantra; it can be anything, phrases like *just chill, it is okay, this too shall pass, nothing is permanent, you are stronger than this, fight it out,* and many more. We must know how capable we are. We all, you and everyone else out there, have the power within us to keep everything balanced by just watching our thoughts.

We are capable of reframing our thought patterns and are able to see things as they are. It is highly recommended to have a mantra, as it will calm you down, improve your concentration, and give you a great understanding of how your mind works.

CHAPTER XXII

DESIRE, IMPULSE AND FREEDOM OF CHOICE

We know how to fix someone, we know how to fix a problem at work, and we are great at counselling someone else, but when the matter comes to us, are we really trained? Do we really know what we want and what we don't want? Do we really know when to act and when to stay silent? Do we know what freedom actually means? These three things are different, but they overlap and are interdependent with each other. And these are the things that really shape us. It is always better to know what we want and what we don't want, when to say and when not to say, when we are acting on our senses or when we get uncontrollable, and how our mind is utilising our freedom. And to be on this balanced path, we must have control over our emotions because negative emotions arise only when we don't get what we want. We have to first think about what we should want and what we shouldn't. Why? so that we would prefer the good and shun the unpleasant. Simply listening to your body is insufficient because our desires frequently take us away from the right direction. The next step is to look at our motives, or the urges that drive us to act. Are we doing just with our actions? Or do we behave because we haven't stopped thinking? Or do we feel it is the right time to take action? We can see things clearly and appropriately when we apply reason, the greatest gift from nature. Although these three are separate training areas, they are actually interrelated and deeply interwoven. Just as our judgements dictate our actions, our wants influence our judgement, and vice versa; however, we cannot simply wait for this to occur. We need to really consider and invest in every aspect of our lives. If we practise this and are aware of our decisions, impulses, and choices, we will achieve true clarity and prosperity and will grow in life.

CHAPTER XXIII

DISCIPLINE AND REASON

There is always a reason for everything. If our lives are not guided by reason, then what is ruling us? Our feelings at this very moment, or our imagination, or our own created assumptions, or a pointless habit of ours? It is really sad how frequently we discover, when we look back on our previous actions, that we were not behaving consciously but rather by the factors we did not even consider, and these are the situations that we regret the most. A mind that lacks self-control and is unaware of its capacity for self-regulation will get distracted by external circumstances and by its impulsiveness. And I am sure you don't want to lead a life like this; discipline is a need. Without discipline, everyone loses control. You are responsible for replacing ignorance and poor discipline with habits. and then you will start acting and behaving differently. And only then you will understand how to control yourself in seeking the impossible, in following short-cut paths, and indulging in unnecessary things.

CHAPTER XXIV

DO NOT GIVE A DAMN

The truth is, no one cares about you. You are the creator or destroyer of your destiny. Do not give so much power to external beings or situations as to ruin your peace or trigger your anger. Situations arise, and they will arise whether you want them or not. Things cannot always go according to our plans. Stop giving a damn about what the circumstances are, because they are not giving a damn to you. If they are doing what they want without caring what you can go through, give them the taste of their own medicine by not reacting at all.

If you think being sad or angry can make the situation turn out according to you, you are wrong. They will not respond as per your wish, so if things are not working out the way you want them to, change your perspective on evaluating the situation and see the difference. Stop cribbing and complaining about the situation; stop getting angry or upset when life hits you because the situation doesn't care about your reaction. They are testing you, so pass the test with flying colours because your emotional turbulence or your stress will not have an impact on the given situation as they are designed in a way where they are incapable of caring for your feelings, your anxiety, happiness, or sadness.

CHAPTER XXV

DO YOUR JOB

When I say this, *I don't care what you think about me; I don't overthink; I see things as they are; I only think about things that are in my control; I don't think about what will happen tomorrow; and I don't care if other people hate me*, the only reason is that now I have learned to keep things simple. Each day gives us a full opportunity to think, think, and overthink. But if we have adapted the mindset of keeping doing our job, rest will fall into place and we will attain peace. At every moment, just focus on one thing; don't bombard yourself with thoughts. Just focus on what you are doing, giving yourself a break from all other considerations. You can accomplish this by treating every task as the only thing to do, letting go of all your distractions, emotional subversion of logic,drama, vanity, and complaints about not getting your desired chance.

You can see how leading a prosperous and pious life is made possible by having mastery over a small number of things. Finding clarity in what you are doing is the right bet. A simple life is a beautiful life. And you can only make your life simpler by moulding your reactions to different situations. A healthy mind is crucial for leading a simple life. So life is complicated, maybe. But don't you think your perspective and take on life play a major role in deciding how complicated your life is? So keep it simple, do your job as best as you can, and fly high and touch the sky. haha !!

CHAPTER XXVI

DRAMA AND ATTENTION

Life will never be without drama. Life has its own ups and downs; there will be sunny days, and there will be rainy days. We all go through situations where there is no problem of ours, but the environment is toxic. There might arise situations where, irrespective of how understanding and empathetic you are, matters of other people will start affecting you. It can happen that, because of the work-life imbalance, you might feel stressed. It is hard to focus on yourself and think well when the situation is not what you have planned for. It is really difficult to be optimistic every time and see the good in everything. But the fact is, no matter how much we all try to avoid such stuff, we have to encounter it in our lives. There is no escape route for this. But when these situations arise and we do not have any control over them, we can still choose to respond wisely. No one is forcing us to take every matter to heart and mind and react accordingly. We have the power to raise our guard and choose what to let in. There are many people you encounter in your life, but you don't make everyone your friend; this works like this only. Be selective in what you choose for your heart and mind. Not every situation requires your attention.

CHAPTER XXVII

DREAMS ARE BETTER THAN REALITY

We often find ourselves smiling in dreams, crying in dreams, or finding ourselves in some very unusual situations, but it's just a dream. It's not real. When we have a dream, it feels like everything is happening to us, but in that moment, we have a choice. The choice of opening our eyes and being present in the reality where we are lying under a sheet. It all feels good now because it was just a dream. Just like dreams, most of the things that upset us are an outcome of our imagination, our own story, and like dreams, they're not reality. The visuals, thoughts, situations—everything feels real, but it's all in our heads. Getting upset by our thoughts is like dreaming when we are not asleep, and it feels like we have lost control over our own thoughts. We just need to switch our perspective and understand that we are just living in a dream—a dream that we do not want and that did not happen. The reaction you are having right now is real, but the cause of that reaction is not, and this is how something is created from nothing. So just wake up and don't get busy wondering about the nightmare; instead, be a daydream, making sure you are creating nicer things.

CHAPTER XXVIII

EVERYONE HAS THEIR OWN PATH

When I was an undergrad student, I read a line: '*Men live in accordance with their philosophy of life and their idea of the world.*' This is so true. Every individual has their own beliefs, and they try their best to live up to them. There comes a time when they feel distracted or influenced, but most of the time, they prefer choosing their values and beliefs over and over. It is thus very important to know and understand where your ruling system is coming from. We can only begin our journey when we can claim that we are aware of our abilities to analyse our own minds, we better understand who we are as people, what emotions and situations make us weaker or stronger, and in real life, who we are. Without knowing your own values and beliefs and your own path, you will never feel alive.

We all want to breathe free; we all want to be free. Only a few of us realise that being really free means being aware of our thoughts; awareness is the real freedom. We all may think we are free and making our choices the way we want, but are we really doing the same? Or we are just doing things that we are so used to doing that we forget the difference. The decisions that we take to impress others who do not even care—the decision to attend every party even if we don't want to, or to become a slave to everyone or to our own mind. We are so dependent on other beings, be it for our own joy, entertainment, or basic work. There is no slavery present in this world that is more disgraceful than one that is self-imposed and created by us. If we are not able to control ourselves in the choices that we are making, how can we claim that we are able to control other people and their behaviours and situations? Real freedom lies when you know who you are and are able to differentiate between the things you are doing that are necessary and the things you are doing out of obligation or to fit in somewhere. If you think you are free, you are free, but ask yourself: are you as free as you think, or is something controlling you? It can be your own mind too.

We all have different faces for different people. No one is the same everywhere. You are a very different person in front of your boss and a completely different person in front of your family and friends. There are multiple sides of ourselves; there are multiple desires, wants, beliefs, and fears. If we are so full of different kinds of thoughts, just think about the world. How is it? It is more confusing and contradictory. The world is full of different people, and you get to encounter only a few of them. It always depends on us if we want to follow the crowd or if we are happy in our own ways, because those who follow the crowd usually get lost in it. Focus on your internal well-being and on self-awareness because if you walk alone, you will find your own path that is completely yours; only you can be the king or queen of this little world of yours.

CHAPTER XXIX

EVERYONE HAS THEIR OWN REASONS

There is a story behind every person, and there are reasons why they are behaving this way. There is always a cause-and-effect relationship wherever you go. So, before judging, analysing, or drawing a conclusion about a situation, always try to see the perspective of others. I know it's tough, but you will notice how being in that position will provide you with an altogether different approach. When you see the situation as what you would have done if given that situation, you will understand the position from which they are coming. It has other benefits too; it keeps you away from meaningless conversation and discussion on the topic of how someone did something wrong to you every time. There are chances when you will feel that if I were at that place, I would have reacted differently, and that is absolutely right; not everyone has the same intentions. It is just a technique to make you feel better about yourself as a person and to feel good about your surroundings and people, because if you think badly of someone and constantly discuss how that affected you, you will never come out of that loop.

We all think we cannot do wrong; we are not wrong, and we always have our own justification for doing things the way we do them. And yes, it can be said that there are only a few people who do wrong intentionally; otherwise, there are people who think they are right in whatever they are doing. Everyone has their own decisions, behaviours, and reasons. I have seen no one who has said, 'Yes, I have done wrong, even after knowing the consequences'. Just think: if someone is doing something, they have their own reasons; that is good for them, and who knows, it is good for you too! Just imagine how much more understanding, acceptable, and calm you would become if you could just perceive other people's actions as an attempt to do the right thing, something good for them, so that they would be happy. Irrespective of your opinion, whether that person is right or wrong, just imagine again to what extent you will feel good when you begin to see things as they appear, and when you adopt this viewpoint, that will completely change your perspective on others' selfish and aggressive behaviour.

CHAPTER XXX

FIRST THIS, THEN THAT

I had this habit of scheduling my life, planning everything beforehand. It is a loop that goes like, 'Only when the weekend comes, I will relax'. Whenever I bought new clothes, I waited for that one special day to come so that I could wear them. Whenever I had this craving to eat a pie in between work, I used to tell myself, 'You can do all you want to do or eat when the weekend comes'. I am sure most of you guys think like this: if this happens, I will do this; if that happens, I will do that. We always look forward to things when we want to chill, rather than looking inward and being in the moment. We have our own reasons to think like this; we believe that when things settle down or are done, we can celebrate, be happy, and be at peace. But ask yourself: how often does this happen? It does not make any sense; my new kurta that I bought is still there in the cupboard because I never felt like this was the day. My craving for eating pie has now gone because the work is done, but another thing came up during the weekend. Life is like this; it goes on.

Do not wait or hold yourself back from living as you want, for that one day. It is easier said than done, but what is the harm in trying? We can always sit with our eyes closed, we can always observe how we are functioning, we can always turn on the music and vibe to it, we can always go for a walk, we can always wear a new dress, we can always turn off our phone, or we can always try to control our thoughts from going in a negative direction. These are the things that matter; these are the things that will provide us with peace. These are the things for which we are living; these things will give us the time to better understand ourselves and to be happy about that. If you want to be happy and at peace, this mindset of dependency will lead you nowhere. Because that perfect timing never comes. You are the creator of your life; you should have the command to create that perfect time whenever you want. Never be dependent for your happiness on other people and situations; happy people take what comes their way.

CHAPTER XXXI

FIT IN

I am really grateful for all those people who helped me during my tough times and made me realise my worth. I have lost myself searching for people and being available for them according to their mood. But we forget we always have a choice: to move forward, to take a break from everything, and to just concentrate on ourselves because, at the end, it is always us. No one will be there except you. In this world, we are so desperate to make connections that we try to fit in anywhere and everywhere. Being flexible is good, but not at the cost of your self-respect. We change ourselves just because we are trying to increase our connections and because we want to be in a cool group. We try to change our opinions, our likes and dislikes, and our habits because we want the approval of others and to be a part of their group. We, too, want our own circle. But it may look fine at the beginning, but trust me, it is not as good as you think it to be.

We are giving them the power because we have certain wants and desires that we think are only possible when we modify ourselves in order to fit in there, not for our benefit but just for some good moments. And let me tell you, your mind already knows what you are doing, and all these moments are being created because you have lost your individuality, your opinions, and you have given up who you are to receive all this. Do you think this kind of happiness lasts a long time? It doesn't. When you try to change your thoughts, you will realise that happiness is never about following in the footsteps of others; it is never about being like others; it is never about fitting in everywhere. Happiness is actually always about being kinder to yourself; it is always about learning how to live with yourself; it is never at the hands of other people; it is always about you.

CHAPTER XXXII

GIVE YOUR BEST

We often discuss among our friends and families how someone has achieved so much in their lives. How they manage everything. How they are doing all this. If they are our own people, we appreciate them; we acknowledge the hard work they did, the hard decisions they took, and the sacrifices they made. But if they are someone with whom we don't get along well, we often say they had a strong background, they didn't face difficulties, and their luck supported them. We have reasons for everything. But we rarely think about ourselves and the decisions we are making to make our lives better. It is always easy to comment on others, but when it comes to us, there is silence.

Everyone has their own battles; everyone takes their own decision; whatever suits them, you can do so too. If you want to shine, it's in your hands. Hard work and luck both matter, but the most important thing that matters is the inner strength and self-awareness that you have of yourself. What are your values? What are your desires? Everything comes back to you. Everything depends on you. You can be whatever you want by just being in control of yourself. The decision to rule the world or the decision to just sit and comment about others—it all depends on you. What do you want to become? The choice is yours; either be the king or don't care who the king is and live your life to the fullest. Just give your best.

CHAPTER XXXIII

GOOD AND EVIL

The war between what is good and what is evil runs through the heart of every person. Both must exist. Inside every person, there is a side to being good, and there is a side dominated by evil. It is a constant fight about who will win, as they are both dependent on each other. You cannot decide what is good if you don't know what is evil, and vice versa. When we are asked about an opinion, we say what we think is good and right, but when it comes to us, and we are responsible for taking action, we do the opposite. It is said that situations change with people, and so does action. Your perception of your friend's action is different from your perception of your actions in that same act. You have to make a choice about which side of yourself you want to give the charge of leading your life; it all depends on your perception. Because this war between being kind, being empathetic, being forgiving, being grateful and being jealous, being rude, being negative, and being sadist will go on and on. But the best part is, every time you and only you will get a choice to decide which side you are on.

So to solve these conflicting desires and attitudes of yours, take a moment and try to know, Why do you think like this? Is reacting that way important or are you just overthinking it? Is that person really making such an impact in your life? Ask questions like this. Because you get a lot of time with yourself and your mind. Make your thoughts a friend of yours. You will notice how different kinds of thoughts are occupying your mind and the level of contradiction that you have to go through every single day, but it's all worth it. As now, you have stopped working against yourself and have started to work for yourself, for your own good, for your own peace.

Never let anything go to your head. Be it success or failure. Always try to be a person who does good to people without having any intentions of harming them. It is not at all tough; life is designed in such a way that we have to constantly fight a battle. You can decide what kind of battle you want to fight. Life is short, and the only thing it wants us to be is kind and a good human being. Never ever change your values and morals for the sake of impressing people. Success is capable of making you arrogant, but always remember that greatness comes from humility. Be confident about your values and your choices, and do everything with good intentions, as no one looks good when they try to make someone else bad.

CHAPTER XXXIV

HAPPY MORNING

Oh God! I am late again. It's already 8 a.m. Why, why am I so lazy? Why can't I get up early in the morning? Why does this always happen to me? I really want to get up early in the morning and create a morning ritual of my own. I fail every time. But the question is, why do I want to get up early? Haven't we felt that the day feels different when we get up early? We have a long day, more time, and more energy to perform our daily routine. and additionally, we get more time for ourselves. I am not saying, do not have a good sleep; sleeping is important. That is the time you surrender yourself; you surrender your thoughts and let your mind and body relax. But yes, it is advisable to go to sleep early and wake up early. We are all aware of the saying that; *early to bed and early to rise makes a man healthy, wealthy, and wise.* It is true. Many successful people have a morning ritual. Some prefer meditation, some exercise, or some journaling.

For me, journaling really works. Here I am able to channelize my thoughts and process them clearly, where I write down my fears,hopes, thoughts, and the things I am grateful for. You must thank God every day for the life you are leading; never take a breath for granted; thank your family and friends who are always there for you; and thank yourself for fighting the battles of life so gracefully. Meditation is not at all easy, but if you practise, nothing is impossible. Meditation really helps to relax and calm our mind, promoting mindfulness and healthy lifestyle choices. Just try to sit with yourself for 5–10 minutes without any gadgets, people, or even thought—just you and your breathing. You will feel great. Exercise is also like this, as it releases chemicals in the brain like serotonin and endorphins that completely change our mood while at the same time improving our sense of control,coping ability, and self-esteem.

The point of developing a morning ritual is nothing that you must follow;the only point is, it just starts your day on a good and positive note where you are taking some time to reflect on yourself. Taking this time for yourself is required in this fast-paced world. Try to build a habit, starting today, where you will spend some quality time with the most amazing being, that is you, where you will get to know what goes on in your mind, what are your exact thoughts, why you think what you think, and how to let go.

CHAPTER XXXV

HAPPY NIGHT

Before going to sleep, review your day. Instead of thinking about what someone said or what should have happened, think about your behaviour and your role in the day. There may be times where you feel neglected, ignored, or alone, but try to give it a different perspective and see why you feel that way because you might be attached to someone or some situation, and they are not. Understand who your people are. I often say this to myself: people like me don't have people; we are the people that people have. There are many kinds of thoughts running through our minds when we go to bed. What did I do today? Why did I say this? Any positive things I learned today? How can I improve myself? And the list goes on. Actually, this habit is necessary, as it gives us clarity.

Keeping a constant watch on ourselves and our thoughts gives us a direction to move forward strongly. Instead of looking outward and analysing other people's behaviour, try to know yourself. You will soon realise your worth and also about them with whom you are surrounded with, it might be thoughts or people or circumstances. Keep your own safe space and take your time to consciously recall the events of the day and notice your emotions. What made you happy and what distracted you? Write down the things you want to work on and say them aloud, *I am not mad at anyone for anything they ever did to me.* Learn to let go. Know your worth and be kind. Make an effort to record your thoughts every day, and you will soon be able to track your progress.

CHAPTER XXXVI

HAVE A SAFE PLACE

Having a safe place of your own is a must. It can be your room, your favourite place, or anything where you feel yourself, where you are not pretending to be anything, where you are true to yourself, where there are no fake emotions, no mixture of thoughts, no filters, and where you are yourself. And this is the best place to be where you are interacting with yourself, asking yourself about your needs, wants, likes, dislikes, feelings, and everything in between. But the busier we get, the more we work, the more we are engaged in learning and growing in life, the more we are busy fighting the battles of life and facing the challenges; it may seem like everything is going well, but something is missing, and it is us. We are so busy with our lives that we forget to spend time with ourselves. And this ignorance creates a problem: it builds up stress, we get confused, our mind does not work properly, it gets overburdened, we forget what's important, and we lose control of our lives. and why does this happen? This happens because we are ignoring ourselves. We are doing great, but at the cost of our peace. We are so distracted with the concepts of success, money, and fame that we forget we are the ones who have the power to get us close to everything we want.

It is very important to take breaks in between, to spend time with yourself, and to create a safe place of your own. Investing time in yourself is the best thing you can do. Being in your safe space boosts creativity, builds mental strength, helps you recharge, makes you more productive, calms your mind, gives you peace and happiness, gives you time to think deeply, helps you relax, and the most important thing it does that is really required in this fast-moving generation where everyone is busy running is that, your safe space helps you to discover yourself again. Healing is possible when you are in a safe space that feels nurturing and allows your feelings to be what they are.

CHAPTER XXXVII

HAVE CLEAR INTENTIONS BY KEEPING YOUR JOURNEY AND END IN SIGHT

Have you ever thought you were just moving without any purpose? Think deeply. You must have something that is keeping you alive, that is letting you move. Everything has an end, so keep that end in mind. We should know where we are going. I am not talking about having any goals. I am here talking about having a value system, having your own philosophy, having your own way of living, and having your intentions clear. If you are making an effort, make your effort with an end in mind. Do not ever use someone as a means in order to meet your ends. Clarify your intentions because it is your false conceptions and false behaviours towards people that make them crazy. If you know what you are doing, never ever hurt someone else's feelings by giving them false hopes and importance. People always respect those who are honest, honest with their feelings, and honest with the other person.

By keeping an end in mind and following it with full honesty, you will understand where you need to stop. It is not guaranteed that by keeping an end, you will get there, but not keeping an end will definitely cost you. Thus, know yourself and know what you want—be it happiness, laughter, peace, a good job, your own startup, or anything else. Just know your thing and keep moving forward; you will definitely land somewhere, and yes, don't forget to keep your intention clear.

CHAPTER XXXVIII

HOPE AGAINST HOPE

Hoping and not acting in favour of our hope can make us vulnerable. I used to think, Why am I not at peace? I want to be at peace. I want to meditate. I want to feel free. But these thoughts of mine were my desire, and in order to get this desire, I am not doing anything. Just constantly thinking about it and hoping to be at peace someday is only making me more stressed. Because here, I am hoping to breathe but not letting myself breathe. Desire of anything, be it peace, wealth, or position, will subjugate us because the value that we are putting into it is not letting us feel free. We must feel content; we should think freely. Our desire exposes us to danger. When we wish for something, when we hope against hope, when we have the opportunity to do something, when we think of being in peace, when we try to be happy, we set ourselves up for disappointments. Because our destiny is always capable of interfering in between, and when it does and our life doesn't go according to our plans, we are thrown in a position where we might lose our self-control. Breath free, live free without setting any limits, and whenever situations arise where you want to do something or feel something, ask yourself: *Are you in control of them or are they in control of you?*

CHAPTER XXXIX

I DONT'T KNOW IT ALL

Socrates said, '*The only true wisdom lies in knowing; you know nothing*'. It is better to accept that you don't know everything. I mean, it is a fact, right? No one can know everything. We all lack something. We are not perfect beings. There is nothing like perfection, and true beauty lies in imperfection. If you really wish to improve yourself, then be ready to accept yourself as you are and say aloud what you don't know. Don't pretend to be someone else, as they are not you. One of the most powerful things about someone in this generation, where social media has taken up our lives, is that the only thing we can say is that we don't know or are not aware of this. There is newness every day. The majority of society seems to have adopted the belief that everyone must be aware of every current situation happening in and around the world; everyone must be aware of the popular television shows; one should know which business has gone up or incurred a loss; one should know where that event is happening; one should watch the news religiously and present themselves to others as a well-informed and worldly person. However, where is the proof that this is really required? Don't take this the wrong way.

My only point is that people are so involved in these things and the feeling of being in the limelight that they create such external pressure on themselves to make their image as someone who knows it all. You must have a general duty to inform yourself about the events that are happening in your family and affecting your country, but that's about it. Don't stress, and learn to say 'I don't know'. You are not a robot; just think how much time and energy you waste in the media, news, reels, what is happening with that particular person, what they are wearing and eating, where they are going, and other things that should not even bother you.

Just observe the difference. How much more at ease and engaged would you feel if you weren't captivated and angered by every scandal, viral tale, and potential crisis? It's okay to not know everything. Take care of your well-being and mental state. You do not even realise how much the consumption of social media and not-so-important news is damaging your mental health. It throws you in a loop—a loop of stress, comparison, low self-esteem, and whatnot. So be confident and don't pretend to know something you don't. Socrates only said true wisdom comes to each of us when we realise how little we understand about life,ourselves, and the world around us.

CHAPTER XL

I WOULD LIKE TO SAY SOMETHING

Having an opinion is a great thing. There is a huge respect for strong-opinionated people. But giving your opinion everywhere does no good. We can have an opinion about everything and still have the power to hold no opinion about a thing and not let it upset our mood. We do not get upset by things we don't know. Don't you think there must be some things where we should remain quiet and act as if we know nothing? The strong are those who admit that they know nothing. Just think about it: do you get stressed thinking about the stuff you don't know about, like what someone said about you behind your back, what mistakes you make about which you have no idea, and things about which you have no idea? You do not stress about these things because you don't know about them. It makes you feel good to have no opinions on this because you are not even aware of the fact in the first place.

It is not possible to have no opinion in most of the things in our day-to-day lives, but having no opinion in most of the things can solve most of our problems. Opinions about things that do not matter to us. It is possible to hold no opinion about a negative thing that happened in the way you didn't want it to. Having an opinion on everything triggers our emotions. It gives rise to conflicts, frustrations, arguments, and mental disturbances. Practise the ability to have absolutely no thoughts about something; behave as if you don't know what happened; you have no idea what happened; it doesn't matter to you; and see the difference. What is happening in someone else's life is none of your business; it is not important to take part in each and every conversation. Everything is not that important; you are giving importance to them. Let it become nonexistent for you and see how little impact it is having on you now.

CHAPTER XLI

INTERPRETATIONS

When I used to study logic, I came across ambiguous statements. Ambiguous statements are those that can be interpreted in many ways. I remember an example: 'I saw a man on a hill with a telescope'. This is a simple statement, but it has more than one meaning. It can either be interpreted as 'there is a man on the hill, and I watched him with my telescope' or there is another meaning: 'there is a man on the hill, and he has a telescope, and I am watching him'. At that time, it really came out as an interesting topic. In life too, there are instances where we interpret the given situation in the way we perceive it, but it can have many interpretations. A word or a statement can have multiple meanings. The words can have a good meaning or a bad one. Something said sarcastically holds a very different meaning. The words hold a lot of power in themselves; they have the power to ruin our mood. It is thus very important to understand what is being said without adding biassed assumptions to it.

Ask yourself: *When someone says something, in which direction do you find yourself?* Do you think they meant something bad, or do you take everything on a positive note? So the point is, if you are a person who wants to be happy and peaceful most of the time, then make sure you are interpreting what is being said in the positive light. Think of what good you can interpret from this, and as a result, you will be at peace. But if you want to get irritated, then interpret things as negatively as you want. The choice is yours.

CHAPTER XLII

INVEST WHERE IT'S WORTH IT

Most of us are shopaholics, but we must spend where it is necessary. It is very important to know the difference. I have seen a video where I learned that the rich are those who invest in creating assets, and the poor are those who keep themselves stuck buying materialistic things and creating liabilities. We are so used to investing and spending on stuff that does not add any value to our lives, if we think about it in the long run. I remember, I had 500 rupees, and I wanted to buy a self-help book, but I thought, What would be the use of it? After reading it once, it will hold no value. On the other hand, I decided to buy clothes that I don't remember how many times I wore. And after a few days, I bought that book too. What is the point here? I decided to spend only 500 rupees, but I ended up spending a thousand. If I had decided that the book was the only thing I wanted, I should have gone for it. But because of my indecisiveness, I bought clothes that were not at all needed. So be aware of the difference; it is easy to lose track. Things will cost what they cost, but the unnecessary things that we buy are not worth any price. This theory can be applied to people and situations too, hence know where you are investing and if it is worth it!

CHAPTER XLIII

KNOW WHO YOU ARE

Many of us have faced circumstances where we were asked who we were. But we weren't able to answer it. We never tried to think about ourselves. We are so busy thinking and knowing about other unimportant stuff and what everyone else is doing that we keep forgetting about ourselves. I have a different perspective; if something comes to mind, it must be important for me, which is why it comes again and again. But does it really make any sense? Does this affect our mental health? If the answer is yes, then why is it important if they are harming our peace of mind? Learn to differentiate between if something is helping you to know yourself better or if something is just ruining your time. I remember in an interview, when someone asked me about myself or the things I was proud of, I was blank. I couldn't understand what to say. I just said very general things, but does that make me 'me'? No, this happened because I was so busy thinking and analysing different personalities that I forgot I too have one. Keep yourself busy in knowing yourself; real strength emerges when you start to look inward. Consider this and simply write who you are and what you are most proud of.

CHAPTER XLIV

KNOW WHO YOUR FRIENDS ARE

Not everyone we interact with is our friend. I often heard my parents say, Make friends wisely; they are the ones with whom you spend most of your time. Your friends have a huge role to play in your life. It is a famous quote: '*Show me who your friends are, and I will tell you what you are*'. Keep a close watch on the people you interact with. If you don't pay attention, your peace will be at their hands. You must choose whether your friends are supporting you or are just there and doing nothing. Sometimes talking to a person can heal you; they are your friends, who are always there to take care of you and who provide you with a safe space. But if this is not the case, then you must think about it. Always remember, you are bound to get influenced by people with whom you are spending most of your time. So see who is making what kind of impact on you. It is not about having a bad attitude that in friendship too, you are seeing if this is beneficial or not, it is only about you as a person who is trying to build a safe place of their own in this wide world. It is about who you are allowing to come into your life and what that person is making or destroying.

You will need people in your life, so why not build a group or a team of two or three, where you all behave like cheerleaders to one another, where you all are friendly therapists, and where you can be yourself? So before starting any relationship, ask yourself: *Are they helping you to be a better person?* If they are encouraging you or dragging you down,if they are a source of joy or if you feel a little depressed after spending time with them? Be aware of what is impacting your mental peace and take decisions accordingly.

CHAPTER XLV

KNOW WHY YOU DO WHAT YOU DO

We often find ourselves doing things out of habit without knowing why we are doing them. There are certain habits that we follow without knowing the reason behind them. I remember when I used to solve mathematical problems, I wondered why this equation was happening like this and how it happened, but my teacher used to say *this was how we were doing it for a very long time. So just do what I say.* That day, I learned maybe some things are like this, as they have always done things like this only. But is this really the way? Are we really going on the right path? Just try to find out what the things are that you are doing without knowing why you are doing them. There is a reason we are studying and gaining experience and knowledge to break the old, same path followed by the crowd and to create our own new path with full awareness of our thoughts. Be curious, ask questions, and do things for the right reason instead of following the crowd blindly.

CHAPTER XLVI

LEARN

There are many things that we don't know, and there is nothing to feel sad about. There is not a single person who is perfect. If you think you are perfect, then you are making yourself believe something that you know is not true; you are being self-deceptive. If you think you know all of it, then there is no point in learning. And it is a fact that you can't learn a thing about which you had some preconceived notions; that notion will always hold you back from performing your best. If you consider yourself perfect and not a continuously growing individual, then you will always find yourself at fault because there are many things to learn about. Respect, kindness, and loyalty are also things that must be learned. If you already consider yourself a person who knows how to respect and be kind, and you are perfect in that,there isn't any scope left for learning. But do you think learning should ever stop? We have this one life, and we have the choice to learn as many things as possible, and learning behavioural traits is a basic thing that is going to benefit us forever in our lives. Learning always keeps us going.

CHAPTER XLVII

MONEY MONEY MONEY

The rich class, very different from you and me, a completely different lifestyle, surrounded by brands, can afford anything they want: luxurious cars, hotels, jets, world tours, and whatnot. We are all moving forward in life, keeping in mind that yes, we need money. Money is important, and no amount of money is enough. Every day we feel, in some way or another, how different our lives would have been if we had money. Yes, it is true. With money comes great power; with money comes freedom; and with money comes happiness. Oh, wait, is it so? Happiness really comes along with money; yes, it can, but only when we are clear—clear about our thoughts, clear about our purpose, and clear about our intentions. It is a sad fact that when we die, we cannot take any of the wealth that we have created in this life; it all stays with our loved ones. And it's nice; nothing feels greater than doing something for people. But if we think that money can solve all our problems, then I am sorry to disappoint you; it is not like this. If you are not happy with yourself, nothing can make you happy. That is why it is said to keep your eyes on the stars and your feet on the ground, look inward, and fly upward.

There are many people out there who have money, but they are the ones often taking therapies. Why so? because they thought that money was the only thing they needed, but money only marginally changed their life. It doesn't seem to address the issues that those without money tend to believe it will. The reality is that no material possession can solve all your problems if your own mind is not ready. External things can't fix your internal things. We forget this and ignore our mental peace and well-being, leading to more pain, confusion, stress, negativity, and whatnot. All riches have their origins in mind. Wealth is created in your ideas and your mind. Take care of yourself and what you think.

Money surely makes a difference, but it will not make a difference if you are still struggling in the vicious cycle of life. You will wonder why someone earning less than you is happier than you. This is because they have a strong hold on their thoughts. So yes, money makes a difference, but it cannot buy you your peace of mind, and to have a peaceful mind, you have to work on yourself, and then only it will make a difference.

CHAPTER XLVIII

MORNING RITUAL

Are you ready for the day? Are you prepared to deal with all that's coming your way? Have you made yourself understand how you are going to react today? Have you given yourself a description of what can happen today? In short, are you prepared to deal with the people? If not, make this your morning ritual so you can be prepared to deal with what is coming your way. The moment you get up, try to sit for a few minutes with yourself so you can tell yourself how you are going to perform today. Your day is an upcoming movie where you are responsible for taking charge of whatever is going to happen.

Tell yourself: '*I am going to meet very different kinds of people; some will be ungrateful, some will be rude, some will be nice and cheerful, some will be judgemental, some will be liars, and some will be loving and fun. All kinds of people are there, and they are like this because they are still ignorant about the difference between good and evil, but I understand what these are and how one should be. I know the bright side of being good and the ugly side of being evil. And these are people just like me. So no one has the power to harm me or push me to be like them. Because I am aware, I know whatever is happening within me. I know I am encountering people who are ignorant; it is not their fault; they will learn soon. I cannot get angry at them or someone very close to my heart because that's not the way it will work since the world needs cooperation and there should be empathy and respect towards each other*'.

These are just a few lines that you can remind yourself of, not just because you want to be prepared for the day and not just because you are trying to create a mindset, but because you don't want to react when things like this occur, as you have prepared for it, changed your perspective, and now you will be able to act with patience, understanding, and forgiveness throughout your day.

CHAPTER XLIX

OBSERVE AND LEARN

Why do we listen to great influencers, people who are successful, and people who are living their lives? because they give us a different perspective altogether. Their way of thinking is different and has something unique. Their way of life, their thought process, and their mental activities are different. They have a unique take on life. We must learn from them—what they run away from and what they seek out. Having inspiration or motivation is crucial. Who that person will be for you depends on you. It can be your parents, cousins, seniors, or any public figure. Most of the time, by observing people, we get to know a lot of things, including how they have the ability to inspire others, have a clear set of values, and have the potential to fight any battle that comes their way. They can be a source of inspiration, support, and motivation. Just keep one thing in mind: true leaders are those whose thoughts empower us and do not overpower us. Be aware of your thoughts while watching the wise.

CHAPTER L

OBSERVING AND PERCEIVING

It has been repeated many times that you are the one responsible for your mood. Situations or people don't have any power in themselves to make you feel the way they want you to feel; it all depends on you. Your judgement defines what you are going to feel. You decide your response; you are the actor in your life. I have read a distinction in a book about which I mentioned earlier, where I understood that there is a difference between our 'observing eye' and our 'perceiving eye'. The observing eye is responsible for 'what the situation is, it sees things as they are' . And the perceiving eye, on the other hand, sees what things mean to us, and that is why it becomes subjective. So the cause of our irritation is the perceiving eye. The event holds no power on its own. It is objective. But when we begin to analyse the event, we give the command to our perceiving eye, which in most cases brings disturbance to our mind and becomes the cause of stress and unhappiness and never provides the space where we are able to see things as they are and see what we can do to make this better. It always adds spice and chutney to events, which can have a negative impact on our reactions.

Hence, the perceiving eye sees more than what is there and adds additional meaning, whereas the observing eye sees events as events without exaggeration or distractions. It depends on you to what extent you want to give control to your perceiving eye in relation to your observing eye, considering scenarios keeping in mind what is under your control and what is not.

CHAPTER LI

PEACE IN CHAOS

In this world, it has become very important to manage and think through our emotional reactions. By giving ourselves time and by being aware of our thoughts, we can bear all kinds of situations. The world is full of people and full of emotions. The world is full of companies, jobs, and work. In the middle of this chaos, we are the soldiers standing up and fighting every day for ourselves. For the love we deserve. For the appreciation we deserve. It is our duty to guard our perception and emotion; it is only our duty to watch what we are thinking. Whenever you get upset, just ask yourself, Is this really the life you have dreamt of? Is this really the environment you were made for? Is it necessary to crib over everything? Is it necessary to cry over work problems? Is it necessary to get angry at almost everything that didn't work out the way you wanted it to? No, right, nothing is bigger than you, and nothing is stronger than you. You and only you are the creator and destroyer of your own life and well-being. Don't waste your time on these matters; every time you get upset, a part of you leaves your body. Make sure to smile, be kind, and just let go. Breathe and move on. Getting upset is normal, but holding it for a longer period of time only breaks your heart. Every time you get upset, ask yourself, *Is this worth giving up your joy?* I am sure the answer is 'no'.

CHAPTER LII

PEOPLE PLEASING

We do things that we don't want to do to impress people we don't even like. Why do you need to impress other people? Why can't you just be natural? Why are you not confident that people will like you the way you are? Why do you want everyone to like you? Is there anything more disheartening than the extent to which we will go to win someone over? Is there anything more upsetting to do in order to make people like us? We are changing ourselves for those people who, I guess, are not so important to us. They are just a part of our lives, and we will just coexist. If we like doing something for people, it is absolutely okay. It is our love for them. But if we are changing ourselves and expecting a response that they will like us and that they will involve us in everything, then it is of no use.

You can't get someone by changing yourself; the real people will love you for the original you, where you can be happy, sad, vulnerable, or whatever you want to be without thinking about what they will think about you. Stop pleasing everyone; pleasing people can become a habit, and the only person that will get affected is you, so instead of being afraid of losing people, be afraid of losing you.

CHAPTER LIII

PLAN

It is so much fun to go with the flow. It is so much fun to just drive without knowing your destination. It feels good when you just roam around the city. But when it comes to life, how does it feel to be unplanned? Most of you are doing great, are following a path of your own, and are happy with it. Some of you are doing great in life but are not happy because you never planned for it. And some are just wondering if they have any plans or not. The last one is sad. I was there when I didn't know what I would do or what I wanted to do, but things fell back into place, and they always do. Planning keeps us sane. Planning provides us with a framework, following which we can move forward confidently. You can travel anywhere and drive anywhere because Google Maps is there. You will never lose your way as long as you have a plan for using it. Just like that, we must have a direction to go in. When you plan a trip, you decide everything beforehand. Unexpected circumstances may arise, and life doesn't always go according to plan. Your plans may fail, but at least you will be in a better position to deal with the situation. It is always better to have a plan than to get lost in your way.

CHAPTER LIV

SELF–AWARENESS

81

It is not always advisable to trust our senses. We think what we want to think; there are only a few people who have the ability to control what they think. It is thus advisable not to listen to everything that your mind tells you to. Our senses are our analysis of situations; they will always be biassed. Self-awareness, in psychological terms, is the ability to recognise that we are separate from other people while at the same time also recognising and assessing our own thoughts, feelings, and beliefs. It is our ability to evaluate ourselves. But real self-awareness lies when we analyse situations objectively, without our own biases. If we indulge ourselves in biassed evaluation and projection, then our senses will perform accordingly. So before delving deep into your own thoughts, develop the ability to question your own instincts, patterns, and assumptions.

CHAPTER LV

SELF CONTROL IS THE REAL PLEASURE

You need self control in an out of control world- James C. Collins

We are young, bro. Just try this once. You will feel great. Have it, take it, and enjoy. You only have one life; live it like there is no tomorrow. Enjoy as much as you can. Make memories. Do it, try this, and what more? Many of us have faced these situations when we are thrown into some addictive habits that we regret doing later on. The peer pressure is real; to struggle to fit in a new place or a new group is real. We are made to do certain activities that we are not comfortable with, but we still do them. But the harsh truth is, we can't blame others because it's their way of life. You are the one getting influenced, so it's you and not them. Self-control is a difficult thing; it is very hard to take a pause at that very moment and then go with our decision. A person who diets is really practising self-control, but the moment they have their cheat day, they eat, eat, and eat. But what happens now? Do they feel happy? No, because each cheat day they eat and hate themselves afterward. Because now they are aware of the aftereffects, they know what happens when they overeat. We often find ourselves at a crossroads where we regret what we did.

It is thus your responsibility to guard yourself from being carried away by such temptations. Like with any impression,once you sense pleasure, resist the urge to act on it right away. Instead of reacting at the very moment, give yourself a moment to think. After that, analyse both events, the one where you loved the pleasure and the second where you regret it and blame yourself. You would then feel very happy, proud, and satisfied with yourself for reaching your goal of refraining completely. But when you are about to take action, resisting the temptation gives you real pleasure, and later in life you will realise how much better it is to be aware of things and how it feels great to be in control of yourself. I always wanted to try smoking, but thanks to my one and only friend, who never made me try this, he knows the trap. He is into it, and let me tell you, he regrets his decision. He didn't take the right action, but he made sure I did. He is on the verge of quitting his habit, but it's tough. We all must realise that it is important to know the aftereffects before getting carried away by temptations. Temptations can be of anything, materialistic or non materialistic, emotional or physical.

Once we understand that indulging in such activities might actually be worse than being away from them, we will realise the importance of self-control, how it is the real pleasure, and how temptation of any kind is regret. It is always better to think before we act; it is always better and more peaceful to live a life without "what if I haven't said that? or "what if I haven't done that?" Trust your mind; make your mind the boss, not your emotions, not your immediate physical sensations, and not your hormonal wants. Just focus on your intelligence and chill; after all, you are a wise person.

CHAPTER LVI

SLAVERY RESIDES UNDER MARBLE AND GOLD—Seneca

We want to live free, we are working day and night to earn our freedom, to live freely. Freedom is a necessity. We may think that celebrities have so much money. They are living their lives, but when we think there are things that they can't do whenever they want, they cannot express their own opinions in front of everyone. Their single words can impact their whole career. They cannot eat the way they want. They have a diet and protocols to follow. They are giving up their freedom in order to get to that place. And getting to that place is not at all easy. They have to behave in a certain way even after knowing they are not like this. They are stuck in their own, created world. We can be free in everyone's eyes, living our best possible lives, but still, we know we are in jail. We only know our reality.

Everyone's life has its own pros and cons. Let's just work hard to live without restriction, but it's really hard. We are going to have boundaries forever in our lives; some boundaries will be our own construction, and some will arise as a by-product of the work and relationships with which we are associated. But under all of these conditions, we can decide how much freedom of ours we are willing to trade.

CHAPTER LVII

SOMETHING BRINGS SOMETHING

Nothing comes alone. If you have accepted someone as your life partner, it is your duty to accept them with all of their flaws. There is nothing in life that is free; it will not come your way only for good. Everything comes with a price. Everything we do has an underlying effect. If you are thinking that when you start working and earning, you will have fewer problems, then you are wrong. You must keep yourself ready to experience the dark side of your happy world. If you become successful, then you have to deal with stress and problems. If you want to be successful, then you have to deal with a lifestyle where discipline and hard work are at the top. If you have a public personality, then you have to deal with gossip and rumours. If you want to be in a happy relationship, then you have to go through fights, disagreements, and frustration. If you want to be rich, then you have to deal with people who are trying to be your friends because of your money and status. So in short, a successful career and relationship will bring their share of problems and stress for you. And you cannot ignore them, but you can be prepared; you can change the way you think and deal with them while at the same time enjoying the place that you have created for yourself.

CHAPTER LVIII

SOMETIMES THE ONLY THING THAT IS HOLDING YOU BACK IS YOUR OWN MIND

Just think about the things that keep crossing your mind, that have become like a nature of you, that keep telling you—I am feeling scared, tensed, lost, lazy, and whatnot. And slowly, these thoughts occupy your mind and control you. Have you guys thought about why it is difficult for us to think about happiness, peace, gratitude, and such positive attributes, and why it is easy to think about their opposites? The reason for this can be that our brain has a natural tendency to give more attention to negative experiences or thoughts than positive ones; this is popularly known as the negativity bias, which causes people to focus on one bad thing in a field of a hundred good things. And the reason for this is, people are so distracted and have low self-esteem because of social media, posts, what other people are achieving, how celebrities are living their lives, and many more. These are external distractions, and we can have the power to limit all of them, but what about internal distractions?

We must understand that we are getting distracted from external events because we are not internally stable; we are internally distracted by our own constructed fears, anger, expectations, lust, greed, and low self-esteem. Every human being is pulled by these distractions, which can likely become our habit if we do not take action and push ourselves harder. Pay attention to your thought patterns and build your value system so strong that nothing can have the power to distract you from going against your values. And paying attention requires work and awareness, and don't you think working on ourselves and being aware of our thoughts are a lot better than being attached to distractions?

CHAPTER LIX

THE WORLD CAN CONTROL OUR BODY, BUT WHAT ABOUT OUR MIND?

We are so aware of our physical selves that when people touch us inappropriately or touch us just by mistake in a crowd, we instantly feel the touch. And something happens in our minds. We feel uncomfortable when someone tries to touch us at a party or some other place. But what happens to us when we ourselves give the right to other people to play with our minds, leaving them disturbed and troubled? We don't like when people push us, touch us, or try to control where we go and what we do. But we are least bothered when someone is doing the same thing with our mind. We have involved our mind and our mental functioning in any random thing. Be it phones, social media, or what other people are thinking or saying, our mind is in control of these outer things. We try to sit down with ourselves, but soon we find our hands scrolling the screen of our phones. When we are with friends or families, it is a basic manner to just be present there talking to them, but most of the members are busy with phones, either uploading photos or clicking pictures in the name of making memories. When we go for a walk, instead of enjoying nature, we enjoy judging the people that are around us. We are never at peace; we are constantly engaged in some or other activities.

We do not even know that this habit has developed within us, and what we used to do intentionally has now become a habit that is unintentional. We don't even know we are doing all this because we have become so used to it. Using phones, thinking about others, and getting affected by seeing other people's lives have become as normal as eating our food. We don't realise how much time we are wasting on this and how unproductive these activities are. And the most amazing thing is that no one is forcing us to look at our phones every time; no one is forcing us to think about what other people are doing; these are all self-created. The weather is not in our control; we can fall down; it's not in our control; but our mind and our thoughts are in our control. Our mind is ours. We must take care of our minds and control our perceptions, as this is the most expensive and precious thing we have. Take care of your mind, and it will take care of you.

CHAPTER LX

THERE IS NO FREE LUNCH

We are so good at judging people accurately, but are we really that good at assessing ourselves? We often hear how important balance is—a balance where we neither see ourselves as more than we are nor value ourselves as less than our true worth. This is an ongoing battle that you have to deal with all your life. But it is a necessity to judge yourself accurately. Knowing your weaknesses can be a great strength, if you think about it. If you are aware of your weaknesses, it will do no harm to you but will make you more prepared. When we make our monthly budget, how accurately do we work? So why not estimate ourselves so accurately? Admitting your weaknesses requires a lot of strength. Learn to judge yourself honestly; there is no one except you who can judge yourself so accurately. Knowing yourself and accepting yourself is the beginning of all wisdom.

My Mama used to tell me that there is no free lunch. And yes, it is true. There is nothing in the world that is free; everything has its own pros and cons. Everything is related; if you think someone is giving you free food, there is a motive of theirs behind this. If someone loves you, there is a reason for it. Nothing happens without a reason. And the sooner we understand this, the better it is for us. Even shopping costs us more than we actually think. So before making any decision, ask yourself, Do I really need this? How much is this costing me? Is it really worth it? What is its utility? You have a long way to go. Be prepared for changes and aware of all the hidden costs that you are accumulating while moving forward in your journey.

91

CHAPTER LXI

THINK BEFORE YOU ACT

Have you ever felt that sharing your pain with others makes you feel better? I am sure we all think this way. Sharing makes us feel light. But does sharing your pain, your frustrations, and your fears with anyone or everyone make you feel better, or does it do the opposite? Sometimes we are so occupied with our thoughts that we forget our own behavioural patterns. Until we stop complaining, gossiping, and sharing our regrets and uncertain events that have happened to us, we will never learn to move on and let go. If you find yourself in this pattern, just knock yourself up and ask, Does this make you feel better? Is this relieving your pain? or is this leaving a negative impact on yourself and on the people you are sharing your feelings with? The moment you stop repeating the incidents—the crying, the cribbing—you will notice a sudden change in yourself—a better change. You will feel free.

Excessive emotion of any kind is bad. Many people say that an emotion made them stronger, an emotion made them achieve their goals, and an emotion kept them focused. But fueling yourself with some strong emotion like anger is bad. You can never rise high and lead a peaceful life with a calm mindset with such a push from short-sighted emotions. Leading a balanced life is crucial for moving ahead, and it can only be achieved by controlling our thoughts and asking ourselves: What is our driving emotion? Getting angry or reacting to every situation never solves anything. Usually, it makes things worse. We react, we spoil our mood, we yell at people, they react, their mood gets spoiled, and everyone is sad now. No one is in the right state. And the problems remained the same. So before getting angry or before getting inspired by such emotions, ask yourself: is it worth it or are you making a sudden decision? Because taking decisions by being in control of our emotions and not ourselves is not worth it. Think before you act, because self-reflection is the key to personal growth.

CHAPTER LXII

THINK GOOD

Water is so amazing. It takes the shape of whatever container holds it, whether it be a glass, a bowl, or a pond. Your thoughts are like water; they will take the form of the environment in which you keep your mind busy. Why is it said to think wisely? Because of the way you think you get the results. There are times when everything is good, but you don't feel it because you have convinced your mind that nothing good happens to you. We are the ones giving them impressions; it is thus our duty to see what we are giving there. We wouldn't even realise when our negative thinking pattern has become a habit and has begun to impact us. We might wonder why this is happening to me and why I am not happy, but the only reason for this is that your mind has taken the shape of what you frequently tried to feed into it. The content of your thoughts impacts your life, just like the way water takes the form of the container.

If you are thinking positively about everything and every situation and trying to calm yourself down, you will see the difference. On the other hand, if you see something negative in every situation, your mind will adapt this thought pattern of yours. I am sure you must have observed that if you see the good in everything, your mind will work freely without any negative baggage. Your mind, along with you, will smile. But if you hold a negative perspective on life, with each passing day, everything you encounter will seem negative. So think wisely, because the way you think can impact your life, either for the better or for the worse. The decision is yours, so look after the thoughts of yours you are sending to your mind.

CHAPTER LXIII

TO BE GOOD OR TO BE EVIL

The external environment is the raw material that is required in order to make a product, i.e., a good product or a bad one. How do we assess the raw materials? By making judgments. Our judgement about the raw material can make our decision good, or if our judgements are twisted, it will clearly impact our decision. So we can say the essence of good is a kind of reasoned choice revolving around our judgements, our value system, or what we believe in. Everybody wants consistency, but very few are able to adopt this lifestyle. It can only be achieved when we filter our external influence and do not isolate ourselves in solitude. Our judgements, or reasoned judgements, can play a very important role because if our judgements are not based on proper reasoning, we will forever get stuck in the chaos of life.

We wonder how peaceful individuals are who are away from the limelight and enjoy their solitude, residing in a very beautiful place away from the chaos of everyday life. But is it so? We can be the man residing in the marketplace, surrounded by people, fighting for life, managing our daily chores and work, and still be equally at peace. Because ultimately the state of being calm, peaceful, and untroubled is the result of our own choice and how we respond or react to that choice, it does depend on our environment, but the majority is dependent on our choice, judgement, and reaction.

I have observed one thing in life: people who think that they will avoid and will not get involved in the daily stress of people and external events will never get what they want because, as it is said, the problem follows us whenever we run and try to hide. But the moment we change the perspective that, *come on, I will fight, I am all ready to control my thoughts. Throw the balls now,* you will feel different. You will notice that if we try to avoid the disturbing thoughts that cause the problem, we will be calm, peaceful, and untroubled wherever we are. To be good or to be evil sometimes depends on external situations, but most of the time it depends on us and on our reasoned choices, reactions, and judgement.

CHAPTER LXIV

TRUSTING CAN BE A MISTAKE

Have you ever heard someone say they broke my trust? They scammed me. How could they do this? Or have you seen in movies or experienced in real life how a person scams another person by making them sign a document that is not what they have explained to them? A completely different document and takes over everything that the individual poses. Many times, we have seen these cases in families themselves, where brothers are doing the same. Everyone is so busy thinking about how to get rich, how to make someone fall in love, and how to get that project that they forget that all these have a right path, and they don't need to scam others for this by telling lies, creating stupid plans, and playing mind games. But the person who is coming into the trap is at fault. There is no problem with trust. Trust is a basic thing that we must have in our relationships, but is only trusting enough? You can trust someone, but blindly trusting them can create a problem. You are a smart being; how can you let someone fool you? Why have you become so lazy that you have stopped caring for your well-being? Why have you stopped looking into matters that require your attention? Why have you blurred your perceptions of people and things?

You are supposed to be active; you are supposed to think about why something is happening the way it is; and you are supposed to think about why someone is doing something. Engage yourself in conversation with the people who are around you to get to know them better, ask questions, talk to them, try to understand them, and then create a perception. Getting carried away is not a solution; be a detective; after all, it is your life. Cross-checking is important; it does not guarantee that you are free of any scams or traps, but it does one good thing. It will create a place for you where you will have no regrets because you tried your best to keep yourself safe from every unexpected thing. You took your actions, and you kept your guard up. You can still choose what your heart says; you can still go for what you want to do; you can still be lazy; you can still love people; you can still trust people, but just tell them; I trust you, but let me verify. If someone is taking this on a bad note, then it is their problem. Make them understand that your trust in them has nothing to do with what they are doing. You are just taking care of your mental health, so trust people, but always verify for your own good.

CHAPTER LXV

UNDERSTAND AND RESPOND

We often find ourselves so engaged and out of control that we ignore what is actually going on. We are all running here and there as if we don't know what pause means. All of us have become robots. We forgot the importance of clarity and understanding in any relationship, study, or work. As a student, I faced situations where I just couldn't focus on what's going on in the class, and my approach was, 'Just know the gist; there is no need to go deeper and understand the concepts'. This trick worked then, but now, when I look back, I realise how wrong I was. Getting concepts conceptually clear feels altogether different. Sometimes we are so lazy or afraid to ask questions in order to get our doubts cleared that we remain confused without clear knowledge and understanding. Asking questions and getting clarity and a deep understanding of situations, theories, and people is required. Asking questions is the first way to begin change.

Without understanding, we reply half-heartedly, and this hampers our relationship. I think understanding something before responding is important. It allows for a deeper connection and better communication. And the biggest problem in communication arises when we do not listen to understand; we listen to reply. And wherever you go, understanding is the first thing that you need to have in order to grow. It is advisable to verify, understand, and then trust anyone; trusting without knowing what they are saying will only affect your thought patterns. Grow slowly; there is no need to hurry. But grow with a clear mind and deep understanding, enjoying each and every day.

CHAPTER LXVI

WAIT, PREPARE, JUMP

There are things that you wouldn't have done if you had thought about them. There are people in our lives who speak less, but when they do, they make sure they are making an impact. I am not saying being talkative is not good; it is your personality, and it can be anything. What is being said here is that you should be certain in whatever you say because it is always better than speaking without thinking or doing an act without giving it a thought. It is very easy to just act, to just roam around, to go wherever you want, to invest anywhere, but it is harder when you have to use your mind, when you have to take a pause to think about what you are going to do. It is okay to take a rest and think about your actions and what is going on during that period. Wait and prepare yourself for what is coming your way. Analyse your thoughts, try to be friendly with your mind, and never react based on your emotions. Whenever you find yourself in such a situation, it is okay to take a step back and bounce back more effectively. We should evaluate ourselves as we do others; we are not perfect beings; we can make mistakes; we must be aware of ourselves and act accordingly.

CHAPTER LXVII

WHAT HAS HAPPENED TO YOU SHOULD STAY WITH YOU

I had this habit of talking to everyone about everything that was going on in my life. I used to repeat the same stories, the same past friendship tales, and the same experiences, most of the time negative ones. But when I paused and thought about it, I realised, Why do I constantly try to remind myself about those events that have nothing to do with my present or future? If this is impacting me so much, what would happen to the person with whom I am discussing this? Think about those people with whom you share everything without having that strong connection. It may look like they love listening to you, but the reality is the opposite.

Your stories may seem interesting to you, but it is not always the way you think. It is also not good for you to discuss your life inside and out with every other person. It may feel good that you are the one leading the conversation, but how do you think it is for everyone else? So live at present and connect to people where there is a two-way street. Listen to them; don't be a performer where your duty is to entertain them with your own stories. It is good to talk to people, but one must know when to talk, with whom to talk, and what to talk about.

CHAPTER LXVIII

WHEN CAUSE MEETS EFFECT

I always wanted to explore the domain of counselling. While going through the internet, I found out about Cognitive Behavioural Therapy. It is a form of talking therapy that can help us manage our problems by changing the way we think and behave. It helps us to recognise what kind of destructive patterns are taking place in our thoughts and behaviour and how one can turn them in a positive direction. This is a simple yet difficult method. Here, you have to act as an observer. You have to listen; you have to pay close attention to the conversation and observe what is being said and what kind of effect it is having on you. You have to recognise how your actions are influencing your thoughts and emotions.

Everything seems easy when you keep things simple without complicating them. You can always become the observer of your own thoughts and actions that are having an impact on you. You are in your control, so you can do this task. By looking into the patterns, you will realise whether the kind of thoughts you are getting are constructive or destructive, whether they are releasing happy hormones or the opposite, whether they contain any biases of yours, and like this, you can frame your questions according to the thoughts you are getting. But only when you perform this activity where you are aware of the time, when your effect is knowing about their cause will you be able to break the negative pattern and move ahead, improving your life.

CHAPTER LXIX

WHOEVER WE ARE, WHEREVER WE ARE, WHAT MATTERS IS OUR CHOICE

We all come from very different backgrounds; some are born rich, some are really trying hard to change the league of their family, some are trying but are not succeeding, some want to change their career path, some people have already established family businesses, and some people are somewhere in between. Everyone is in some place, maybe a high or a low, but in each place, our freedom to choose what we want and what we will do, can be maintained if we wish to exercise our power. The situations don't always come in our favour; they might be advantageous or disadvantageous for us, but in all the circumstances, as already mentioned several times, we have only one thing to work upon, and that is our choice. Our lives are full of ups and downs, and our lives are full of uncertainty. We might be at the top when we were eighteen years of age, or we might be at the bottom in our twenties. We might succeed in our thirties; anything can happen, but the only constant thing is our freedom to choose—the choice of response, the choice of thought.

Everywhere and anywhere, it's not them; it's only you. Life is simple. It will constantly ask us in any of our situations, What are you thinking? What do you want? What is the next choice? Are you making the right choice? It all depends on us and how we choose to respond to life.

CHAPTER LXX

YOU ARE NOT ALWAYS RIGHT

How often do you think your plan has been executed the way you thought it would? How often do you think that the person you thought to be kind and trustworthy is just the opposite? How often do you decide on something and, as a result, don't get it? We all suffer from these kinds of situations. And they arise because we are so confident in our judgement that we don't even realise,it is actually dependent on our preconceptions and biases. These are not facts, but we still think we are thinking the right way. We often, in order to support our judgements, try to give arrogant opinions without understanding the whole picture. And think of ourselves as so smart. But as time passes and we get involved, we observe what has actually happened or is happening. Then we question ourselves: Why haven't I thought about this before? Why did I trust them? Why was I so rigid in my plans? Why did I convince everyone without knowing the full picture or without listening to anybody? Don't you think it is not a smart decision to wait for the reality check?

And the other thing is, have you noticed that when it comes to money, you become so careful. When someone asks you to lend money or give them change, you check every detail before trusting them. Nowadays, the shopkeepers check the notes to see if they are real or fake. So why are you not sceptical about your decisions in other matters? Why do you trust people easily in matters that don't involve money? It is really important to be sceptical about matters related to ideas, thoughts, and assumptions.

Hence, we must remember that we are not always right, we can make mistakes, we must admit that we don't know this, and we must admit that we are not as smart as we think we are. Smart individuals are those who are not afraid to cross-check themselves, who are not afraid to ask questions and get their doubts clear; smart individuals are those who know what they are doing and why they are doing it; smart individuals are those who are considerate, who are ready to listen, and not those who think they are right every time.

CHAPTER LXXI

YOU CAN BE A GOOD PERSON AND STILL SAY 'NO'

We spend so much time pleasing other people that we forget how little time is left for us. We indulge ourselves so much in people and their problems, pointless grief, foolish joy, greedy desire, and social amusements that we forget we are passing our time with no purpose. I believe one of the hardest things that I faced in life was saying 'no'. 'No' to invitations where people are just inviting you for the sake of inviting and do not have any love for you; 'no' to a request where I felt trapped in people's emotions; 'no' to a person who is just using you because they do not have anyone else. Sometimes you know all this from within, but still, you are with them because you are afraid of saying 'no'. We can say 'no' to our emotions; we can say 'no' to anger, overexcitement, greed, lust, and obsession, as these are all traps. I can understand that saying 'no' can hurt some feelings; they will think you are rude, but you will soon realise that the more you learn to say 'no',the better you will understand people and yourself.

Being a 'yes man' makes you a pleaser, and we are not ice creams, giving anyone the right to lick us when they want. Learn to say 'yes' to the things that matter to you, where your presence is felt, and where you feel happy. This will let you enjoy your life to the fullest on your own terms around people who genuinely love you.

CHAPTER LXXII

YOU CAN BE THE BEST VERSION OF YOURSELF

There are many people in this world who know a lot more than you, who are smarter than you, who dance or sing better than you, who are very well-read about the events going on in the world, who earn more than you, and who have something that you don't have. Or it can be said that no matter how successful or smart you are, there is always someone who is smarter, more successful, and wiser than you. So do you think there is any point in comparison? Comparing yourself with others does no good. It will only affect your mental health; you will never feel content or okay with yourself. You will keep yourself so busy comparing yourself with others that you tend to forget the fact that no one is like you. You have a unique personality and can do wonders. This is the one side of the story where you were busy comparing and forgot that you are beautiful too.

There is also another side to the same story where an individual is so full of themselves that they look down on people and think of them as useless. We have seen people who are so arrogant and rude and have a superiority complex that they think they are the smartest and wisest and the wealthiest person born on earth. No one can beat them. But as I said, they should not forget that there is always someone who will be better than them.

So the lesson learned is: be the best version of yourself; do well; do good to others; you are good; you can do good.

Superiority and inferiority complexes are the same thing and can have the same impact. A balance is required. But trust me, if you know yourself, if you know your strengths and weaknesses, if you are aware of yourself and your surroundings, if you are happy with who you are, if you are just not going in life but growing in life, then you are safe from both of these complexities.

CHAPTER LXXIII

YOU CAN BE WRONG TOO

I remember a girl who is so full of herself that she hardly thinks she is at fault. I had a chance to spend some time with her. I used to like her a lot, but soon I realised what she truly does. She plays the victim card in front of you, bitching about people and believing that she has done nothing wrong; the fault is always with the other person. I used to believe her, but when I observed, I realised nothing is ever one-sided. The person she has a problem with confronted her and accepted her mistake, and then everything was chill between them. After a few days, she did the same to me, and I too went there because I am a kind of person who believes that I can be wrong; no one is perfect, and I want to know where I did wrong that has made you behave the way you do. But there are other kinds of people like them who are always ready to accept when someone apologises to them, but they never think they can be wrong too. Their actions can hurt people too. I believe it's a life where we will make mistakes, where we will sometimes say mean things to people we don't even mean, where we do certain things that are inappropriate, but it is never too late to say sorry and accept your mistake if you are truly wrong.

We are all free agents; we have to stop taking things personally. If someone is saying something, we must listen; it is their opinion. Not everyone is our enemy; sometimes a person can say something to you about you as a person that you weren't aware of. So don't be like the person who never feels they can be wrong too, who tries to control you as they wish, who acts as if you did wrong to them. Accept your mistake with dignity and pride, but don't chase people. I made that mistake. But I don't regret it, as my intentions were pure. I believe it is mentally and physically exhausting when you are the only one trying to fix a relationship that requires effort from both sides. I tried to save every relationship, but I realised I was losing myself trying to please everyone. And I don't want that. I accepted my mistake; I tried, but it didn't work out. I decided to let go, and now I am at peace, without any regrets that I haven't tried.

CHAPTER LXXIV

YOU EITHER CONTROL YOUR MIND OR IT CONTROLS YOU—Napoleon Hill

Our mind is the most powerful tool existing that has the power to either make us or break us. Everything has certain functions to perform and has some unique qualities; so does mind. We have to train our minds to perform only those functions for which they are so well designed and to ignore all the other functions and things that can produce negativity and impact our mental health. It can be our best friend or our true enemy. It completely depends on us what we want it to be. The proper function of the mind is the exercise to approve or agree to something, to accept what is in our control, and to understand what is not under our control, and why we should stop thinking about that. It gives us the motive or the cause to perform something; it acts as a guiding principle that makes us aware of our priorities. It prepares us to make or construct something for our journey, for what lies ahead, and to deal with circumstances where anything can happen. It sows the seed of hatred or dislike towards something, and we must pay attention if that repulsion is towards negativity or bad influence or if the brain is working just opposite of it. It also has a role to play in what we desire or crave, and it should be the desire to do better every day, better than yesterday, and to do our best. This also has the power to reject or deny things that may have a negative impact on us, like the feelings of lust, anger, and greed. And the greatest function that it has is the power of choice—to choose the possible course of action, to do and think right. This is what the mind is here to do; anything except this is a distraction, which is not good for our mental well-being.

CHAPTER LXXV

YOU HAVE THE POWER TO UNDERSTAND AND VALUE IT

Have you ever wondered if you are able to draw a conclusion about a situation because you have that power of understanding within yourself? If this wasn't the case, how would you analyse your things and other matters? You are studying, working, having a conversation, presenting your works, caring for others; you are capable of learning the meaning of each and every thing; you are able to find out the reasons why things are working; you are a learning creature who can grow and learn as much as you want. All this is because you have that power—the power to understand yourself. By using that power, you have the chance to improve yourself and make yourself a better person. It is an ability that everyone has, but not everyone is so lucky to utilise their power of understanding to the maximum level.

We are the beings that have reasons and logic on our side to make arguments, convey a judgement, or decide a conclusion. So don't you think we should be grateful for this? Only because of this understanding have we got some responsibilities that are keeping us sane and helping us to make a presence in this whole wide world. Just try to spend a moment today realising that you are privileged to be able to make decisions based on reason and logic. This offers you incredible authority to change both your own and other people's circumstances. Being grateful is a wonderful thing; you can feel the sudden shift to happiness and peace.

CHAPTER LXXVI

YOUR ADDICTION IS NOT YOU, BUT IT FEELS LIKE YOU BECAUSE YOU'VE SPENT SO MUCH INTIMATE TIME TOGETHER. – Toni Sorenson

We do many things that we regard as harmless or think of as not having a negative impact on our lives, but are they really not affecting anything? To be precise, I am not only talking about smoking addictions or drinking addictions. Addictions can be of many types. Someone might be addicted to gossiping or talking about other people's lives; someone might be addicted to coffee or tea; or someone might be addicted to continuously checking their phones. Have you ever felt that if you have a habit of drinking tea in the morning or afternoon and you don't get it, you feel restless? Have you ever thought that the only day you are not getting your tea makes you anxious, and the moment you have it, your headaches vanish? It happened to me. I knew tea was not good for my health, but still, I considered it harmless and continued to consume it until the day I realised how it was managing me, not me, who was deciding whether to have it or not.

We humans never realise that these harmless habits are running our lives until we begin to introspect or look within ourselves and understand our choices and the impact of those choices. We are so used to checking our mobile phones that we don't realise we are slowly becoming addicted to them. Some people are so addicted to negativity that they, without even noticing, begin to see that in every instance. The same applies to gossiping. So it is high time to pause, take a break, and be aware of the things you have surrounded yourself with and see, if you are controlling them or the situation is just the opposite.

CHAPTER LXXVII

YOUR OPINION IS THE ONLY THING YOU SHOULD THINK ABOUT

There are several things that we can control, like our choices, our opinions, or everything of our own doing, where we are the sailor of our ship. We cannot control what other people are thinking about us, what my grades are, about our position, or anything that has nothing to do with ourselves. People are going to dislike you if they want to, and teachers are going to give you bad marks irrespective of you being good. So why to worry about these things that do not involve us, where we have no role to play? So try to control your opinions about the event that has just occurred, be it good or bad. You will notice that your opinion on the event is making an impact on your mind the way you want it to. You cannot control the situation, but you can control what you think about it.

I remember when I was making a loss of 20,000 rupees when I started my journey of investing, and yes, I do not have a lot of money,I am a small-town middle class girl , so I was stressed. When I told this to my mama, he said only those people can make such a loss who have the guts to do wonders and who have invested so much to experience such a loss. And the market is not in your control, so do not worry; you will bounce back. At least you are learning the power of patience and uncertainty. My Mama always has his ways to calm me down. So this incident completely changed my perspective on looking at the event.

Every single thing that is not under our control, like the outside world, other people, luck, etc., still has the power to ruin our peace, but it depends on us how we deal with them. Try to see things as they are and make yourself realise that all I have is my mind, and the moment I begin to think about what other people are doing and why this incident happened, I don't feel good. Observe that it all begins with you. Your happiness is just a thought away, so train yourself to look inward, to know yourself, and to be aware of what you think and how you think. Because it all begins within you.

CHAPTER LXXVIII

YOUR REACTION TELLS A LOT

It is always our own opinions that fuel emotion within us. I consider someone my friend, and I stand by her whenever she needs me, but she doesn't feel the same for me. She ditched me when she met other people. I felt hurt, but am I making the right choice if I am thinking of confronting her? Our reaction to this situation will decide whether we are being ditched or not. Act normal; it is just a situation that happened, and it is good that you know who is going to be there. But reacting to it will do no good. I made this mistake. I wish someone had told me this earlier. If we feel that someone has betrayed us, that they did wrong to us, then this emotion—an emotion of anger or sadness—will occur in our minds. But if we try to control ourselves, a lot can be saved, and most importantly, your mental peace can be saved because now you know how to not get carried away by such incidents, and with time and distance, you will notice the amount of self-control you have learned. Our reactions always depend on people; the way we react to our friends, the way we react to strangers, and the way we react to family are different. So if we have so much awareness of how to react to different people in different situations, why aren't we making ourselves aware of our reaction and not our response in the very first place? Why aren't we taking a pause, regardless of knowing our own reaction is the real source of distress?

If you feel like your loved ones or your colleague have done you wrong, let it be. You can feel the urge to give it back to them, but don't do it. This is not you. Write down what you felt wrong, write down what they said to you that hurt you, write down your expectations, and write down everything by keeping in mind they are going to read it. But never send this letter to them. Keep it at your place. It is easy to yell, it is easy to fight, and it is easy to let people know what you are going through. But you will always end up with regret. Because now too, when things don't work out in your favour, the outcome does no good; it just worsens the situation. Try to keep your anger to yourself by writing it down and seeing the relief. And I am sure you will feel nicer and happier as you have now learned to maturely deal with situations instead of just reacting.

CHAPTER LXXIX

YOU CAN CONTROL YOUR CHOICES, BUT YOU CAN'T CONTROL THE OUTCOME OF YOUR CHOICES. – Howard G. Hendricks

Have you ever thought that most of the time we are busy thinking about stuff that does not actually matter, that does not make any sense, that has only one thing to do, and that is ruining our mental peace? Take a breath and give yourself a chance to look within yourself and be aware of your thought patterns. Choices are your own; perception is yours, so make the best of them, something that does not hamper your mental stability. If we think about what happened and what could have happened, we are just passing our time with zero productivity. Instead of delving into these kinds of loops, we must try to invest in ourselves and what is better for us. Does thinking about them make me feel better? Does thinking about that incident that happened some years ago help me out? Does thinking about why they behaved the way they did and why you reacted in that way help you out? You can always refer to your past incidents to learn from your mistakes, but being there will give you nothing but anxiety and stress. Just be in the moment because you have full control over your choices. Keep your intentions pure, and do not worry about what the consequences are because they are not in your control.

Know the difference between what you can change and what you cannot change. Stop wasting your time thinking about things that you do not have any control over or influence over. Just pray to God to give you the strength to differentiate between what is important and what is not and to accept things as they are. It is just the beginning, and one day will definitely come when you will be immune because now you are focusing on those activities of your day where you have control and thus making your choices wisely.

CHAPTER LXXX

WHEN LIFE THROWS LEMON AT YOU, MAKE A LEMONADE

There are many problems coming your way. You have to deal with lots and lots of emotions. If you are a person who takes everything very seriously, then you should learn the art of dealing with stressful situations. Because the world does not behave as per your wishes. There might be situations that you thought would end up like something else, but they turned out completely opposite. And you are stuck there. You are not able to understand the situation or find the right approach. And you consider yourself weak and bad at dealing with emotions? But is it really so? Who is the most powerful being in the world? It can be you; the most powerful person can be you if you are the one controlling your thoughts and if you do not get upset by anything that is outside your reasoned choice.

Most of the time, people are unhappy because they have expectations. Try to live a free life and see the difference. The problems are uncontrollable; they will come. Uncertain situations arise, but we can always be in control of our senses by being aware of our impulses. Do not run from your problems; face them with dignity and grace. It will only make you stronger. People will poke you, and situations will shake your confidence, but learn the art of being powerful, strong, and invincible. Invincibility is just a word, but it gets power from your determination, your reaction, and your understanding. We choose to react; we make things important, wonderful, ugly, or whatever we wish them to be. We give meaning to everything. So prioritise things wisely. We can easily handle pressure or difficulties and can brush off rude attacks. So instead of saying 'why me', just say 'try me. I am way stronger than this'.

I have read a quote from Helen Keller: "*Your success and happiness lie in you. Resolve to keep happy, and your joy and you shall form an invincible host against difficulties.*" People who know how to control their impulses are great; don't worry, you will learn it too. Just try to know yourself because impulses of all kinds will come and go. You don't have control over the impulses, but you can control your part. And your job is to control them and channel them in the right direction. Think before you act; think before you say something.

Ask yourself: *Why are you behaving this way?* We often regret thinking about the way we handled the situation in the past, but it's never too late. It is great that you understand this now. Move forward and always respond to situations using the lessons you learned from your mistakes. You cannot control the situation, but you can always control yourself. Always keep in mind that when life throws thorns at you, hunt for roses.

CHAPTER LXXXI

CAN YOU SIT AT ONE PLACE QUIETLY ?

I always found it difficult to sit with myself alone—without a mobile phone, without a book, without anything. Just sitting with myself for some time and not doing anything. It sounds easy, but it is very difficult. I learned very hard that not doing anything is also something that we are doing. Sitting with yourself is the best thing you can give to your soul. We are so busy in our lives, wanting to do everything, constantly comparing ourselves with others, and running to get somewhere without having a definite purpose; we are just following the crowd. We are all driven by a compulsion, a work, or any activity or addiction that is not under our control. We are so scared of being still; for us, stillness equals death. But is it so? No, stillness gives us peace.

Simply wait,be quiet, and still. The world will freely offer itself to you. You will get to know yourself better; you will know what you want and what you don't want. We are so afraid of being still that we want to get distracted. We choose to be at war even when peace is the most preferable choice. Hustling is great, working hard is great, and having goals and aims is great only if you are choosing this for all the right reasons. In the midst of all this, invite stillness into your life, because inner stillness is the key to outer strength.

CHAPTER LXXXII

THE ULTIMATE REALITY: DEATH

Death is the ultimate reality; no one can escape it. We all have come; we all must go. There are people who are arrogant, full of attitude, looking down upon people, and there are people crying over little things, never happy, and there are happy people who know the mantra of their way of life; there are people who are always ready to fight; and there are people who need people beside them. In short, there are various kinds of people in this world. Everyone is unique; no one is the same. And you get to choose what you want to become. Because journeys are different for different people as they are in our own hands, but the destination is the same for all of us, for all the different beings. You and the person you dislike will go down the same path to the ultimate destination, death. Enjoy this short time on earth without letting negative emotions control you by keeping your feet firmly planted on the ground and your eyes fixed on the stars. Live and let live.

CHAPTER LXXXIII

FEAR IS IN MIND

Are you scared of losing people? Do you feel people do not like you? Are you putting in a lot of effort in order to get liked by others? Are you scared of getting sick? Are you not happy? Do you think you are not worthy? Do you think that everything bad happens to you? It is all in your mind; fear is in your mind. Everything that you don't want to go through, fear will make sure you will go through the same. We are so scared of some things that, intentionally or unintentionally, we attract the opposite. If you want to be liked by everyone and you are putting in great effort, the opposite will happen. If you keep telling yourself I have no one in my life, no friends, and no one loves me even after giving so much, you will realise these are your hidden fears that have taken over you. And now, in real life, you don't have anyone.

Your fears create an illusionary reality. And you believe it. Think about your thinking because the things we fear or dread, we blindly inflict on ourselves.The next time you get affected by some feeling or thing, just try to control your impulses. If you will not control your impulses, if you lose your self-control, you will be the source of the reaction you so fear. Fear attracts fear. So watch your thoughts, because you never know if whatever you are scared of has a negative impact on you. Knowing your fear is great, but constantly repeating it is not at all great, as everything we want is always found on the other side of fear.

CHAPTER LXXXIV

HOPE FOR THE BEST, PREPARE FOR THE WORST

Your life is never going to be sorted out. There will be problems. There will come situations where you will feel like you don't want to fight, but is this the solution? Not really. There is no one who wants to live a life full of difficulties; there is no one who wants stress; there is no one who wants to go through a work-life imbalance; but these are situations that may arise in your life, and you will have no control over them. You will only get the chance to fight it out. And I know you will fight. You will be considered mad if you crave problem-free living, but at the same time, you will be considered mad if you think there will be no problem in your life. So be prepared to deal with that.

There is a saying, *Hope for the best*. We should always hope for the best. No one wants to hope in a negative light, but what we must be careful about is that if we are hoping for the best, we must be prepared for the worst. Because difficulties will arise, it depends on how prepared you are within yourself to deal with them. The way people are making such nice homes for themselves to live peacefully and happily with their family while at the same time considering the aspects of earthquakes and constructing their earthquake-resistant homes is a nice example we can use in this context. Be as prepared as you get ready for an event where two hundred guests are invited, but you, being an event manager, have prepared for an extra twenty plates.

Pray to God to provide you with so much strength that you must remain in the right mental space, always ready to fight. I know you don't want to experience pain; you want to be free from pain, but be prepared to deal with it if it comes your way, and pray to God to give you so much strength that you could deal with the pain with bravery, with honour, and with courage. I know you don't want to go for a fight, but be prepared to proudly bear the scars, hunger, and other needs if you are chosen to go for a fight. I know you do not want to be sick; you want to lead a healthy lifestyle, but if you do get sick, make sure not to act carelessly or irresponsibly. The only point here is not to wish for these difficulties, but to wish for the strength, the virtue, and the courage that will make your difficulties bearable. And you will be proud of yourself.

CHAPTER LXXXV

PRIORITISE

Know what is important and what is not important for you. Be grateful for the things you have. Focus on yourself and what you're doing. Look what and who are your priorities. If you are not content with yourself or are not satisfied with yourself, you won't be free, but you will necessarily be envious and jealous of any person who has everything that you desire. If you get down to any level, either by planning and plotting against them or by constantly self-sabotaging yourself, you will damage your own worth. But by having a clear mind, you will be in a very good and safe place, you will be in a better relationship with the people, you will praise everything you have, and you will focus better for a nicer tomorrow. Most of the famous personalities who are living the life they dreamed of are the kind of people whose lifestyle is a result of prioritisation. They never disconnected themselves from their roots but still drove themselves crazy in all the right ways. They have interests that are decidedly below their financial means, so any income would give them the flexibility or freedom to pursue whatever they want to do in life. Their unexpected prosperity is just a coincidental phenomenon that comes with great knowledge, understanding, and clarity about what they really want. When someone has such a clear understanding of what they truly love, need, and want, they are able to fully enjoy life.

CHAPTER LXXXVI

TRUST THE PROCESS

True happiness lies in giving up everything that is not in our control. Our decisions, our reactions, our sayings, and our duties are everything that has to do with us, and this anyone cannot take from us. This is all ours. The earth is revolving, and we are no exception; we will revolve around too. Sometimes in our favour and sometimes not, but it depends on our choice whether we are moving towards good or evil. Never regret anything that you have done in the past—making relationships that didn't work out, being in friendships that backfired on you, taking advantage of opportunities that you didn't take advantage of, and many more things like that. All these are bygones; your reaction was under your control, and your reaction is still under your control, so watch your thoughts. Do not make yourself sad thinking about how other people have reacted or should have behaved because it is not in your control. Remember, each day, when you go to sleep, tell yourself—it is the time to relax, surrender yourself, and trust the process. Keep yourself ready to start the whole cycle again the very next day.

Do not confuse your power of choice with the lives of the people you are associated with. Keep it simple and easy because the only choice and the only thing you are controlling is your mind. With time, people realise that there is clarity in simplicity. People in their adulthood think that if they are in the limelight, have many possessions to show off, are winning every time, are all-rounders, and engage in activities that look cool, then they are leading a life one desires, but still they are not happy or satisfied with their lives. With time, they will realise that these are all illusions, and real happiness is attained when they are clear in their mind set, as there is clarity in simplicity. Do not run behind things that you do not want; do not get influenced by people and what they are doing because that is not your calling or your way. Learn to differentiate between your wishes and what the world is doing. It is really nice to get inspired by people and the work they are doing, but do not compare yourself with them because they are following their path and not yours; you have a very different path. So, just try to manage one thing in order to move forward, and that is your will, your choice, and your mind.

CHAPTER LXXXVII

PEACE LIES WITHIN YOU

Do you get easily influenced by looking at people your age doing better than you and earning a lot of money? Do you easily get disappointed in yourself? Do you feel like you are standing nowhere in the world and have developed a habit of questioning yourself? But trust me, believing in yourself and trusting that you are on the right path, that you are worthy, that you are capable of making your own decisions, and that you are enough, you do not need to follow the path of others will give you a different kind of strength. Calmness can only be achieved when you are in this state of mind. Having a clear vision of what you want and what your target is—it doesn't matter how big or small it is as long as it is all yours—can give you peace from within.

Following our own path does not guarantee us success; we may fail, but we will learn a lot and have no regrets. Instead of comparing yourself with others, try to look at yourself and appreciate your actions. If you have a clear idea of what you want, it doesn't matter what anyone else wants, and you will get a hold of your thoughts by not changing your mind whenever you scroll through new information. Peace is thus always associated with ourselves, our paths, and how we are sticking to them by continuously making adjustments without getting distracted by the outer world and by constantly fighting with our inner devil.

YOU CAN ALWAYS RESTART

It is possible to start living again. It is possible to rearrange your thoughts. Try to see things without having any preconceived notions. because that only affects you, not anybody else. We have had our bad days and our encounters with people whom we used to adore, but now things have changed, and it hurts. We have our beliefs about people and their words that do not exist anymore; the feelings have changed, the people have changed, and our feelings towards them are not the same anymore. The person whom you used to consider your friend is not your friend anymore and is living her happy life without you. It hurts right, thinking these things always trigger our mental well-being, where we feel lost,stressed, constantly judging ourselves and their behaviour, analysing what-if scenarios, and whatnot. But trust me,it is fine. It happens to all of us.

But the reminder here is that no matter what happens or what has happened, no matter what our response was, no matter how disappointing the situation was, no matter how things didn't work out, no matter if you are all alone, the reality is that you are still present, breathing in and out. We must try to embrace only good moments spent with the people; we must learn to let go of our evil because bygones are bygones. What happened five minutes ago, five months ago, or five years ago is the past. You are not going that way. Move forward, keeping good thoughts in mind. It is easier said than done, but nothing is impossible. We can restart whenever we like. Restart, reframe your thoughts, do not repeat the mistakes that you made earlier, and keep going.

CHAPTER LXXXIX

EVERYTHING WILL BE ALRIGHT

We have our plans, but what if things don't go according to our plans? Is it okay to cry? Yes, it is okay to cry, but keeping some things in mind, we should not forget that there can be a bigger plan too. If something isn't happening according to our plan, there is no point in blaming ourselves or the situation every time we discuss something, as there is always something bigger planned for you. Nothing can throw you off track. You can be late, but you will reach your destination. There are times when you think of something as a pain or a disaster, but after some days you realise that it turned out to be in your favour. It gave you a break, if not other things. Taking a break requires a lot of courage and strength.

I remember when I had a year gap in my studying career. There were people who tried to make me feel bad about this, or more than people, I was criticising myself, but when I first took a gap year because I was not finding my purpose, I was just living without any aim, then I decided to come back home. I didn't want to waste my parents' money. I was unhappy, but then a very unexpected thing happened. The doctors said my grandfather has cancer and the treatment is not possible here, so my Dadi and Dadu went to my Bua's place in Hyderabad for his treatment. And my parents were busy working; all the responsibilities of the home were on me. My Nani was suffering from dementia; she became like a child. I used to spend time with her. I really miss those moments. So, coming back to the point, I am trying to say that one day it will all make sense. If I hadn't taken that gap year, I wouldn't have had the chance to spend so much time with my Nani. I learned so many things during that time when I was with my family.

It will all make sense one day. Never regret your decision. If you have a plan, God has a bigger plan for you. No one wants to take a break; no one wants to start late in their career; everyone wants the best for them, but not everyone can at the same time get whatever they wish for. There will always be ups and downs in your life. We are humans, and we are unable to see the whole universe. We just see what we are doing and what is in front of us, but there is a whole different universe there that is working—a universe bigger than all of us. Trust the process, and always remember that one day it will all make sense. You are doing great.

It's A Wrap

I hope now it is understood that there is nothing in this world that can hurt you as much as your thoughts. And there is nothing in this world that can heal you as much as your thoughts. Our thoughts have the power to shape our reality. We are aware of the saying that *'beauty lies in the eyes of the beholder'*. So it is the observer's responsibility to see how beautiful they can make their world. Beauty in itself is nothing; we give it meaning through our thoughts and perceptions. It is thus very important to know what our thoughts are like: are they inspiring us or are they demeaning us? Are they making us feel low or making us feel stronger? Are they only considering what is in our control, or are they just going anywhere or everywhere? Are our thoughts in our control, or are we the ones getting controlled by them? Ask yourself questions; try to know what you are thinking and if it is possible to control your thoughts.

Questioning your actions and your perceptions by being aware of them is the first step in controlling your mind. Master your art of perception; know what is under your influence and what is not under your control. Learn how to respond and not react. Understand that there are multiple interpretations of a single thing. If you are not happy with the way you feel, change the way you think. No one has the power to make you feel the way they want you to feel unless you are ready for it. Never give anyone the power over you to bring back the unhealed version of you when you are working so hard on yourself to become better every day.

Self-awareness, self-examination, and self-determination are three very important things that we must adapt to, as they can help us reframe our negative thoughts into positive ones. To be a rational being, we must keep ourselves away from any confusion and meaningless stress, and in order to achieve that, we must look inward, and examine ourselves critically, making our own decisions that are unbiased and free of our own destructive thoughts. It is important to understand that our thoughts are not always right, but they make us who we are. They are influenced by our experiences, our beliefs, and our perceptions. If your thought patterns are self-critical, full of comparisons, full of what other people will think, or if you always wonder what will happen if things go wrong, then watch your thoughts. You become what you think.

Fill your mind with thoughts that calm you, as there is no true success without peace of mind. Pay attention to what you think, manifest wealth, happiness, and love, and spread goodwill and love to others. Think good, do good, and good will follow. Saying it again,note in your mind that *there is nothing in this world that can hurt you as much as your thoughts. And there is nothing in this world that can heal you as much as your thoughts.* So let's embrace the power of our thoughts and choose to make them work for us, not against us. Because it's you—you are the actor, you are the decider, and you are the responder—life is thus always about you and your thoughts.

Thank you for giving it a read. This really means a lot!!

www.ingramcontent.com/pod-product-compliance
Lightning Source LLC
Chambersburg PA
CBHW021541150726
47990CB00006B/2341